D1144511

1

YPRES
1914-15

YPRES
1914-15

WILL FOWLER

First published 2011
by Spellmount, an imprint of
The History Press
The Mill, Brimscombe Port
Stroud, Gloucestershire, GL5 2QG
www.thehistorypress.co.uk

British Library Cataloguing in Publication Data.
A catalogue record for this book is available from the British Library.

ISBN 978 0 7524 6196 0

Typesetting and origination by The History Press
Printed in Malta
Manufacturing managed by Jellyfish Print Solutions Ltd

CONTENTS

List of Illustrations   7
Introduction   11
Timeline   16

Historical Background   19
The Armies   26
      The Commanders   39
      The Soldiers   54
      The Kit   59
      The Tactics   68
The Days Before Battle   75
The Battlefields: What Actually Happened?   81
      First Ypres   81
      Gheluvelt   87
      The Wider Battle   92
      The Langemarck Legend   97
      Nonnebosschen   101
      Relative Quiet   106
      Second Ypres   111
      Gravenstafel   113
      St Julien   122
      Frezenberg   127

	Bellewaarde	129
	The Salient	131
After the Battle		138
The Legacy		143
Further Reading		145
Orders of Battle		147
	First Ypres	147
	Second Ypres	156
Index		158

LIST OF ILLUSTRATIONS

All illustrations are from the Author's Collection, unless otherwise stated:

1 The Menin Gate Memorial to the Missing.
2 Winter sunlight picks out the concrete structure that was the dressing station at Essex Farm north of Ypres where Canadian doctor Lieutenant Colonel John McCrae composed the iconic poem *In Flanders Fields*.
3 The shrapnel-pocked gate of the Cloth Hall at Ypres in 2011.
4 The 1839 treaty, guaranteeing Belgium's neutrality.
5 Lord Kitchener, the Secretary of State for War.
6 German troops advancing along the road in 1914. (The Book of History *–The World's Greatest War, Vol. XIIII, The Grolier Society, New York, 1920; www.gwpda.org/photos*)
7 This card showing 'A street in Flanders' was produced to raise funds for the British Committee of the French Red Cross to provide clothes, furniture, seeds, implements and children's food for French refugees displaced by the war.
8 Belgian and British troops fighting alongside each other in Ypres. (The War Illustrated Album DeLuxe, Vol. 1, Amalgamated Press, London, 1915, Courtesy of the Great War Photo Archive: www.gwpda.org.uk)

9 In 1914 there was optimism and enthusiasm for war when men left for France. By the latter years, when the rush of volunteers had dried up and conscription had been introduced there was grim acceptance that the departure for the Western Front might be a one way trip.

10 A sergeant with his load carrying equipment, rifle and bayonet stowed in the training manual positions.

11 The British 18 pounder deployed during an exercise in Britain.

12 At the outbreak of the First World War artillery was still seen as a close support direct fire weapon and so shrapnel and case shot would be used against infantry and cavalry.

13 Erich von Falkenhayn.

14 Field Marshal Sir John French watches troops who are going 'Up The Line'.

15 Preserved German trenches at Bayernwald; the use of hurdles to revet the trench walls was a typically German technique.

16 A typical British soldier's equipment.

17 The Short Magazine Lee Enfield in the capable hands of a Rifleman who is demonstrating the correct way in which to load a charger (clip) of five rounds.

18 A British officer inspects a Lewis Light Machine Gun.

19 A painting of Corporal Gibbons of the Royal Engineers constructing jam tin bombs in a frontline position.

20 An observation balloon used for spotting the fall of shot for the Royal Artillery.

21 A painting of Private Gudgeon of 1st Battalion, Northamptons who was awarded the DCM for his work as a runner and guide in the First Battle of Ypres.

22 A postcard showing 'A British sentry in Flanders'.

23 The experience and professionalism of the BEF were demonstrated by Corporal Redpath of 1st Battalion Royal Highlanders (The Black Watch) who won the DCM during the First Battle of Ypres in November 1914.

24 Field Marshal Douglas Haig who commanded I Corps at Ypres and would eventually command the BEF.

List of Illustrations

25 The first man from the Indian sub-continent to be awarded the Victoria Cross, Sepoy Khudadad Khan.

26 German prisoners carry a wounded British soldier.

27 Cavalry troops patrol along the flooded Yperlee Canal, Ypres. (New York Times, 03/21/1915 Courtesy of the Great War Photo Archive: www.gwpda.org.uk)

28 As the only survivor of his machine gun section Quartermaster Sergeant Downs of 1st Battalion, Cheshires manned a gun and beat off German attacks in November 1914 until reinforcements arrived. He was awarded the DCM.

29 Lieutenant John Dimmer of the 2nd Battalion, Kings Royal Rifle Corps cleared jams in a machine gun on three occasions but suffered multiple wounds including a round that stuck him in the jaw during fighting on 12 November, 1914 at Klein Zillebeke. He was awarded the Victoria Cross.

30 A cross, footballs and a Christmas tree mark one of the places where the Christmas Truce of 1914 broke out spontaneously.

31 A modern sculpture of an Australian miner in Vierstraat, Wijtschate.

32 Hill 60. This bunker constructed by the Australians is built on top of an existing German structure that had disappeared into the ground following mine blasts and shell fire.

33 The savage fight in the south-east corner of Hill 60 on the night of 20 April 1915.

34 Looking like strange rodents in their P Helmets or Tube Helmet gas masks, a ration party of the King's Royal Rifle Corps is directed by 2nd Lieutenant Edward Allfrey to move through a gas saturated area.

35 Later in the war canaries were used to detect poisonous gases. (BirdsandtheWar,Skeffington&Son,London,1919;www.gwpda.org/photos)

36 Towering over the road junction at St Julien the statue of the Brooding Soldier is a powerful memorial to the heroic fight put up by Canadian troops of the CEF in the first gas attack of the war.

37 The statue shows a soldier with arms reversed - the soldier has his head lowered and his hands resting on the butt of his rifle – the drill position adopted by troops lining the route of a funeral.

38 Rifleman F. Hamilton of 8th Rifle Brigade mans a Vickers machine gun during fighting near Hooge in July 1915.

39 40-year-old Jemadar Mir Dast of the 55th Coke's Rifles (Frontier Force) would win the VC in fighting on 26 April 1915 in the Second Battle of Ypres.

40 A British infantry shelter in Ploegsteert Wood in 2011.

41 In an almost Napoleonic scene near Shell Trap Farm – aka Mouse Trap Farm – men of 1st Battalion, Royal Lancaster Regiment led by 2nd Lieutenant R.C. Leach launch a counterattack and capture a German flag on 24 May 1915.

42 February 1918 – the war has only nine more months to run as this weary stretcher party walks along a duckboard track in the pulverised terrain at Ypres.

43 A grim but evocative name for a little Commonwealth War Graves cemetery near Ploegsteert Wood, a shell-shattered wood known as 'Plug Street' to British soldiers.

44 The caption to this card reads 'Scotties have a clean up after a spell in the trenches'. The reality was that men stank, their clothing and bodies had lice, and it could be an effort to stay clean shaven, let alone clean.

45 Pack mules loaded with shells are led off a 'corduroy road'.

46 A bunker integrated into the German trench system at Bayernwald.

47 Photographed in 1917, Ypres has become a shell-shattered ghost town – however the cellars still provided cover for troops transiting through the town. The Cloth Hall can be seen framed by the ruins in the foreground.

48 An observer in a balloon took this picture of Ypres in 1917.

Front cover: A photograph of troops marching to Ypres, taken in 1917 by photographer Ernest Brooks, depite being taken later in the war this has become an iconic image of the entire Ypres campaign. (Crown Copyright)

INTRODUCTION

At 8pm every day a simple ceremony takes place at the Menin Gate Memorial in the town of Ieper (Ypres) in Belgium. For a few moments before 8pm the noise of traffic ceases and stillness descends over the memorial. On the hour the regular buglers drawn from the local volunteer Fire Brigade step into the roadway under the memorial arch. They sound *Last Post*, followed by a short silence, followed by the *Reveille*. This ceremony has been carried on uninterrupted since 2 July 1928, except during the German occupation in the Second World War, when the tradition of the daily ceremony was kept alive at Brookwood Commonwealth War Graves Cemetery in Surrey, England. On the evening of 6 September 1944 as the Polish 1st Armoured Division was still fighting to clear parts of the town, men from the volunteer Fire Brigade took post at the Menin Gate and in a salute to liberation the ceremony was renewed.

The massive war memorial at Menin is dedicated to the commemoration of British and Commonwealth soldiers who were killed in the Ypres Salient during the First World War and whose graves are unknown. The memorial is cut into the ramparts at the eastern exit of the town, where a fortified gate once stood, and marks the starting point for one of the main roads out of the town that led Allied soldiers to the frontline. Designed by Sir Reginald

1. The Menin Gate Memorial to the Missing. During the First World War this was the shell-shattered gap in the ramparts at Ypres through which many of the men who defended the Salient marched out to the trenches.

Blomfield and built by the British government, the Menin Gate Memorial was unveiled on 24 July 1927.

Its large Hall of Memory contains the names, cut into vast panels, of 54,896 British and Commonwealth soldiers who were killed in action. In order that the names at the top panels could be read from the ground an arbitrary cut-off point of 15 August 1917 was chosen and the names of 34,984 missing after this date were inscribed on the Tyne Cot Memorial to the Missing.

Nearly eight-five years after the Menin Gate was unveiled the memorial and the ceremony still attracts large crowds of visitors throughout the summer. At other times, on a weekday or in winter, the pavements under the memorial can be empty – though that is becoming rarer now. Whatever the day and whatever the weather, every evening the busy road through the memorial is closed to traffic shortly before the ceremony.

Central to the ceremony is a verse from the poem *For the Fallen* written by Laurence Binyon in 1914. It is now known as *The Exhortation*:

They shall not grow old, as we that are left grow old.
Age shall not weary them, nor the years condemn.
At the going down of the sun and in the morning
We will remember them.

Binyon was too old to serve as a soldier but in 1915 he volunteered to work as an orderly at a British hospital for French soldiers, Hôpital Temporaire d'Arc-en-Barrois, Haute-Marne, France. He returned in the summer of 1916 and took care of the wounded from the Verdun battlefield.

The Menin Gate and Tyne Cot are extraordinary memorials – the number of names seems overwhelming, however today any visitor to the Ypres Salient cannot help but be moved by the number of smaller cemeteries dotted throughout the area. Some are obviously the sites of regimental aid posts or casualty clearing stations – the distinctive white headstones are clustered and not in neat lines – the men lie where they were buried, moments after they died, and exhausted doctors and medical orderlies turned to the next wounded soldier and struggled to keep him alive. In some there are headstones with the words 'buried somewhere in this cemetery'. The doctors and orderlies had written down the

2. *Winter sunlight picks out the concrete structure that was the dressing station at Essex Farm north of Ypres where Canadian doctor Lieutenant Colonel John McCrae composed the iconic poem* In Flanders Fields.

names, but the bodies were lost in the mud and chaos of war as artillery fire destroyed both the living and the dead alike.

One of these men who fought to keep wounded soldiers alive was a Canadian Army surgeon. Lieutenant Colonel John 'Jimmy' McCrae MD of Guelph, Ontario was working at a dressing station close to a canal north of Ypres. During heavy fighting in the Second Battle of Ypres his commanding officer recalled that:

> Headquarters were in a trench on the top of the bank of the
> Ypres Canal, and John had his dressing station in a hole dug in
> the foot of the bank. During periods in the battle men who were
> shot actually rolled down the bank into his dressing station.

Along from us a few hundred yards was the headquarters of a regiment, and many times during the battle John and I watched them burying their dead whenever there was a lull. Thus the crosses, row on row, grew into a good-sized cemetery.

from *The papers of Edward W. B. Morrison*

That cemetery would later be known as Essex Farm.

McCrae was not only a dedicated surgeon – and a veteran of the war in South Africa – he was a poet. It was after a particularly grim day that looking out over the crosses marking the graves of the men who had died at the dressing station he wrote the powerful poem *In Flanders Fields*, immortalising the image of fields 'where the poppies blow' marking the burial sites of thousands of young British, German, French and Belgian men who died throughout the Western Front.

Creating the poem may have been an act of catharsis, for the story has it that having written it he crumpled the paper and threw it to one side. A medical orderly recovered it and it would later be published in the popular British magazine *Punch* on 8 December 1915.

Now, the crosses have gone – replaced by neat headstones – but the power of the poetry has remained, commemorated by the poppy worn in buttonholes and made into wreaths for 11 November, when we commemorate Armistice Day, and on Remembrance Sunday. A testament to the fact that the sacrifice of Ypres remains with us even today.

TIMELINE

1914

October 1914	The Allied frontline extends from the towns of Langemarck, Zonnebeke, Gheluvelt, Zandvoorde, Messines to Armentières. The British Expeditionary Force holds the eastern and southern sectors, while the French are on their left and the Belgian Army to the north
7 October	German troops enter Ypres for just a short time as Allied troops are arriving in force
12 October	The Battle of Messines commences (ending on 2 November)
13 October	The Queen's Own Oxfordshire Hussars arrive at Ypres. In the previous day they have seen action in Bruges, becoming the first British Territorial Force unit to do so in the First World War
	Battle of Armentières commences (ending on 2 November)
14 October	A larger British and French force reaches Ypres. The British force, IV Corps, is led by the 7th Division.

14 October	IV Corps headquarters is established at a convent in Poperinge, while its advance headquarters is at the Hotel de Ville in Ypres. The lack of space there meant that part of the town's Cloth Hall is also used. General Henry Rawlinson, commander of IV Corps, is billeted in Ypres	
19 October	The First Battle of Ypres commences (ending on 22 November 1914)	
21 October	Battle of Langemarck commences (ending on 24 October)	
22 October	The Germans begin their concerted attack on Ypres	
29 October	The frontline contracts towards Ypres, with villages like Zonnebeke falling to the German advance	
	Battle of Gheluvelt commences (ending on 31 October)	
31 October	The Germans are pushed out of Gheluvelt	
1 November	The Germans capture the strategic Messines–Wytschaete Ridge	
2 November	The British I Corps and French XIV Corps hold off a major German attack on Gheluvelt	
10 November	The Germans begin their second major artillery bombardment of Ypres	
11 November	Battle of Nonnebosschen	
22 November	The historic Cloth Hall and St Martin's Church are badly damaged by shelling	
	First Battle of Ypres ends	
January	The frontline runs through Bikschote, Langemarck, St Julien, Broodseinde, Hooge, Zillebeke, St Eloi, Wytschaete and Ploegsteert. Despite almost continuous fighting in the winter months, the line has barely moved	

1914

1915

1915	March	The civilian population of Ypres start to return to the town after the previous year's artillery bombardment
	14 April	The Second Battle of Ypres commences (ending on 25 May 1915)
		The Germans launch a renewed artillery bombardment of Ypres, lasting nearly a month during which most of the town is destroyed
	17 April	The British capture Hill 60
	22 April	The first poisonous gas attack of the First World War launched at Bikschote against French troops. Belgian and Canadian troops help the French secure their line
		Battle of Gravenstafel commences (ending on 23 April)
	24 April	Battle of St Julien commences (ending on 4 May)
	25 April	The Germans start their main attack against British positions
	May	Heavy fighting occurs throughout the month and both sides suffer heavy casualties
	5 May	Hill 60 attacked by the Germans and British are pushed back
	8 May	Battle of Frezenberg commences (ending on 13 May)
	24 May	Battle of Bellewaarde commences (ending on 25 May)
	25 May	Second Battle of Ypres ends
	22 July	British forces advance along the Menin Road, near Hooge
	29 July	The first recorded use, by the Germans, of a flamethrower
	7 August	A German gas attack on Allied forces at Hooge takes place

HISTORICAL
BACKGROUND

The town of Ypres has a long history. There are reports that a community on its site was raided by the Romans in the first century BC. It was in the Middle Ages that Ypres became a prosperous city with a vigorous linen trade with England and a population that grew to 40,000. Wealth and prosperity had its drawbacks and the hostile attention of jealous neighbours and rampaging armies made it necessary to fortify the city. Parts of the early ramparts, dating from 1385, still survive near the Rijselpoort (Lille Gate). Work on the famous Cloth Hall that would become a landmark in the First World War began in the thirteenth century. Over time, the earthworks were replaced by sturdier masonry ramparts and a partial moat. Ypres was further fortified in the 17th and 18th centuries while under the occupation of the Hapsburgs and the French. Major works were completed at the end of the 17th century by the French military engineer Sebastien Le Prestre, Seigneur de Vauban.

It was the First World War that would bring the city to prominence. The town had been held against German attacks in 1914 in the First Battle of Ypres and like Malta or Stalingrad in the Second World War, it became of symbol of defiance. Ypres was the last major town in Belgium that had not been occupied by the Germans and so, to the Belgian people, it represented the last part of their homeland that was free.

Prior to the First World War the neutrality of Belgium had been guaranteed by the major powers, including Britain, through an 1839 treaty and so Germany's invasion of the country brought the British Empire into the war. However, Ypres was a strategic position during the First World War because it stood in the path of Germany's planned sweep across the rest of Belgium and into France from the north. The Allies and particularly the British wanted to hold it because it was a key site to protect the Channel sea ports and associated shipping lanes, and a good point to advance from to seize Ostend and prevent the Germans using this port as a U-boat base.

The Schlieffen Plan, the initial German attack on France through neutral Belgium, had ended in failure at the First Battle of the Marne in September 1914. This had forced the Germans to retreat and dig in on the line of the River Aisne where French and British attacks were unable to breach well-sited defences and fighting seemed to descend into a deadlock. In an effort by both parties to regain the initiative, French and German forces made progressive moves northward in vain attempts to

3. The shrapnel-pocked gate of the Cloth Hall at Ypres in 2011 – a small survivor from the ancient building. Little of the original building survives – the structure that stands over the market square was built in the 1920s and '30s.

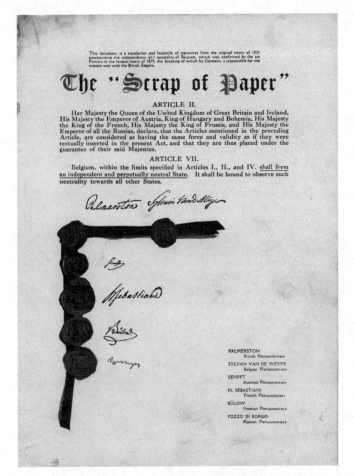

This document is a translation and facsimile of signatures from the original treaty of 1831 guaranteeing the independence and neutrality of Belgium, which was confirmed by the six Powers in the famous treaty of 1839, the breaking of which by Germany is responsible for the present war with the British Empire.

The "Scrap of Paper"

ARTICLE II.

Her Majesty the Queen of the United Kingdom of Great Britain and Ireland, His Majesty the Emperor of Austria, King of Hungary and Bohemia, His Majesty the King of the French, His Majesty the King of Prussia, and His Majesty the Emperor of all the Russias, declare, that the Articles mentioned in the preceding Article, are considered as having the same force and validity as if they were textually inserted in the present Act, and that they are thus placed under the guarantee of their said Majesties.

ARTICLE VII.

Belgium, within the limits specified in Articles I., II., and IV. shall form an independent and perpetually neutral State. It shall be bound to observe such neutrality towards all other States.

PALMERSTON
British Plenipotentiary

SYLVAN VAN DE WEYER
Belgian Plenipotentiary

SENFFT
Austrian Plenipotentiary

H. SEBASTIANI
French Plenipotentiary

BÜLOW
Prussian Plenipotentiary

POZZO DI BORGO
Russian Plenipotentiary

4. The 1839 treaty that Britain, Austria, France, Prussia and Russia signed to guarantee Belgium's neutrality and which would eventually drag them into the First World War.

outflank and envelop each others' armies – this push north and west became known as 'The Race for the Sea', and eventually it reached its destination, with barbed wire entanglements being constructed to the water's edge in Belgium. Repeated failures to outflank the enemy ensured the gradual extension of opposing

THE SCHLIEFFEN PLAN

At the beginning of the twentieth century the German High Command knew that if war broke out between Germany and Russia, France, which had treaty obligations with Russia, would declare war on Germany. In 1905 Alfred von Schlieffen, the German Chief of Staff, drafted a plan to knock France out of the war in six weeks before Russia had time to mobilise. It was based on an attack by 90 per cent of the German Army through neutral Belgium and Holland that would hook south and east and take the German armies to Paris. The remaining 10 per cent of the German Army would hold the line in the east as Russia slowly mobilised. Like so many plans it was predicated on assumptions which on the day were not realised. Schlieffen and his successor von Moltke, who modified the plan by not routing the attack through Holland, believed that Belgium would not resist, that Britain would not be drawn into the conflict and finally that France would be defeated in six weeks – in reality Belgium fought, the Russians mobilised in an incredible ten days, the French fought tenaciously and Britain entered the war.

trench lines as combatants sought cover from machine gun and artillery fire. By the end of 1914 the trenches would stretch from the North Sea to the Swiss border.

In early October the British Expeditionary Force (BEF) relocated from the Aisne to Flanders, on the extreme left of the Allied line, and was ordered to probe north to Ypres. This coincided with simultaneous German moves westward and a series of confusing encounter battles ensued in which the larger German forces pushed the British back to an extended and thinly held line. It was during the relentless attacks on Ypres and its outlying villages between 19 October and 22 November 1914 that the famous Ypres Salient was created.

Initially the only British troops at Ypres were the Queen's Own Oxfordshire Hussars (QOOH) – a yeomanry regiment attached to the Royal Naval Air Service which, as a personal initiative of the First Lord of the Admiralty, Winston Churchill, had landed at Ostend in late August with 3,000 marines and a force of aircraft and armoured cars, in order to bolster the Belgian defence of their channel ports, particularly Antwerp. This force (known as the Antwerp Expedition) was rapidly expanded by two brigades of the Royal Naval Division (RND) and would eventually reach Antwerp only to be driven back on the night of 8 October. Their battle casualties amounted to 195, of which fifty-seven were killed. However, 936 men became prisoners of war and nearly 1,500 men of the Royal Marines and RND were cut off by the Germans. These men eventually managed to cross the Dutch border to be interned in camps. Among those retreating was the poet Rupert Brooke, who was later to die of blood poisoning on a French hospital ship, moored off the island of Skyros, while on the way to the Dardanelles. The QOOH – nicknamed in the British Army 'Queer Objects on Horseback', had been used to augment the Antwerp Expedition with the blessing of Lord Kitchener, Secretary of State for War. The regiment had had a historical link with the Churchill family since 1892. Winston Churchill had become a member in 1902 and his younger brother, Jack, was serving with them in 1914 when they became the first Territorial Force unit to see action. Until the arrival of the British 7th Division they were the only troops between the German Army and the Channel ports.

The Germans actually managed to enter Ypres and a few local surrounding villages, before being forced back onto the ridges around the city by the British 7th Division which, landing at Zeebrugge on 6 October, posed a threat to the German commander, Erich von Falkenhayn's rear.

Corporal Charlie Parke and 2nd Battalion, Gordon Highlanders, 7th Division reached Ypres on 14 October after a punishing speed march of 103 miles in which the last 40 miles had been covered in a little under 40 hours. To the weary British, Ypres seemed as

5. Lord Kitchener, the Secretary of State for War.

peaceful and welcoming as Lyndhurst after a long route march through the New Forest. The quaint old-fashioned Flemish town, lying sleepily by the side of a serene, tree-shaded canal, appeared very remote from war. At every cottage door were rosy-cheeked women with tempting jugs of wine since very few were T-totallers in the British contingent.

The Ypres area has been described as being like a saucer, with the city of Ypres at the centre where the cup sits and the surrounding land to the north and east being the saucer rim. This gives an indication of the advantages of terrain and position that the Germans enjoyed for the greater part of the conflict.

The German Army now surrounded the city on three sides, bombarding it throughout much of the war. In the years that followed, the British, French and Allied forces launched costly attacks from the Ypres Salient into the German lines on the surrounding ridge lines.

In the First Battle of Ypres (19 October to 22 November 1914) the Allies recaptured the town from the Germans. The Second Battle of Ypres (22 April to 25 May 1915) is notable or notorious for the first large-scale use of chemical weapons by the Germans. With the assistance of these frightening new weapons they were able to capture high ground to the east of the town.

THE ARMIES

German

At the beginning of the war the German Army was the strongest in Europe. It had a professional officer corps, good weapons and had learned the lessons of the Russo-Japanese War fought at the beginning of the century. The British and French were to learn to their cost that the Germans had mastered the art of concentrating machine guns in strong points and due to the capture of Lille, an industrial city not far from Ypres, a reliable supply of huge volumes of cement and concrete would allow them to build formidable field fortifications.

However in 1914 the German High Command believed that superior training and tactics would ensure that they would fight a short war and so just 5.4 million men had been mobilised. At the close of the war in November 1918 this figure stood at 13.2 million men.

Just as patriotic fervour had swept France and Britain in 1914, so too in Germany. Some 308,000 *kriegsfreiwilligen* (wartime volunteers) did not wait for their conscription papers and joined up voluntarily. Since many men had been through military service before the war, a large percentage of German soldiers had an adequate standard of training. Though only 25 per cent of the

6. *German troops advancing along the road in 1914. Mobilisation of their forces was a key issue for the German Army. (The Book of History – The World's Greatest War, Vol. XIIII, The Grolier Society, New York, 1920; www.gwpda.org/photos)*

kriegsfreiwilligen were trained reservists, it is a myth that the German soldiers who fought and died in the First Battle of Ypres were young untrained student volunteers – the so-called *Kindermord bei Ypern* – the murdered children of Ypres. Of the German forces committed to the Battle of Ypres, the majority were experienced and well trained.

Despite careful staff work and planning in August 1914 German mobilisation did not run smoothly. Thirty-one trained infantry divisions reinforced fifty-one active divisions. In addition, four *Landwehr* (home defence) and six *Ersatz* (replacement) divisions were formed. On 16 August, six new reserve corps were created. Five of them: XXII Corps (containing 43rd and 44th Reserve divisions), XXIII Corps (containing 45th and 46th divisions),

The German Soldier

Though there was a core of regular officers and men, the Imperial German Army, like the French, relied on a conscript force. Call up for young men was seen as a patriotic duty and while training could be unimaginative and often brutal it ensured that there was a large number of men who had been recently trained or were undergoing training. Regiments had regional or state affiliations which ensured a close bond within these formations. Like the British there were elite cavalry and Imperial Guard formations and officers were drawn from titled families. This produced a straightforward attitude to authority which until the latter years of the war was accepted without question. Some of these aristocratic officers were highly competent and well trained, although others were guilty of expending the lives of their soldiers in hopeless attacks and counterattacks. For the average soldier in his teens and early twenties – younger than the men they faced in the First Battle of Ypres – it was a case of 'follow my leader' and once low-level officer and NCO leadership had been removed, as in the fighting at Gheluvelt in 1914, morale and cohesion could collapse.

In 1914 the Germans shared the same optimism as the Allies and were confident that their superior training and equipment would ensure that this would be a short war. They, moreover, had the precedent of history to back this conviction. The Prussians had soundly defeated the French in the Franco-Prussian War and had made a serious study of the staff work required to support the strategy of war in Europe. In this new war they were confident that they could do it again and men marched off to fight garlanded with flowers and the embraces of their loved ones.

XXVI Corps (containing 51st and 52nd divisions), XXVII Corps (containing 53rd and 54th divisions). Attached to these were the 9th Reserve Division, the Marine Division and the 6th Bavarian Reserve Division. Owing to the nature of mass mobilisation, the German Army struggled to equip its divisions. In lieu of helmets, *shakos* (military caps) were obtained from the Berlin Police and weapons from training units. By September, weapons shortages were so acute that captured Russian and Belgian small arms were being used to equip reserve divisions.

The reserve divisions had only nine field artillery batteries instead of the twelve assigned to regular divisions. The artillery personnel in these reserve divisions were also not as well trained as in the regular divisions. Moreover, they lacked telephones or means of communication. The principle German field gun was the 77mm that fired a 15lb shell and according to the pattern of gun had a range of between 5,800 and 11,700 yards.

At Ypres the Germans deployed two armies: the Fourth commanded by Field Marshal Albrecht (the Duke of Württemberg), which comprised five corps and the bigger Sixth Army under Rupprecht Crown Prince of Bavaria which contained eleven.

French

Like the German Army the French had a carefully worked out mobilisation plan in place in 1914. Reservists were well trained since from 1905 men had undertaken two years of training and from 1913 this had risen to three years. The expectation was that 5–13 per cent of men would not be mobilised immediately. In the event only 1.5 per cent did not report to the Colours. In France there was a passionate desire to avenge the defeats and humiliation of the Franco-Prussian War of 1870–71 and recover the territory lost to Germany.

The 1911–13 cohorts (those born in the years between 1891–93) were already serving when war broke out. The French called up the 1896–1910 cohorts in August 1914 and the 1914 cohort in

7. *This card showing 'A street in Flanders' was produced to raise funds for the British Committee of the French Red Cross to provide clothes, furniture, seeds, implements and children's food for French refugees displaced by the war.*

September 1914. By the end of 1914 they had called up the 1892–95 (born between 1872 and 1875) as well as the 1915 cohort. By spring 1915, an incredible 80 per cent of all French males between the ages of eighteen and forty-six had been called up and France eventually mobilised 45 per cent of its male population, more than any other major belligerent. The French Government also reduced the grounds for exemption from military service. The French called up 82 per cent of all men eligible to serve in the last decade before the war. This was in sharp contrast to Germany, which called up only 59 per cent. However, this was offset by German manpower reserves being much larger. Although, the French were also able to draw on a pool of indigenous troops from their North African territories.

The main field weapon of French artillery was the modern Canon de 75 modèle 1897. The gun was used by both field and horse batteries and was capable of firing twelve to sixteen shells per minute and under pressure a well-trained crew could actually fire thirty rounds per minute. The design was so good that it would soldier on into the Second World War. In many ways it reflected the philosophy of the French Army in 1914 – manoeuvre and attack. The army deployed some 618 field and twenty horse batteries, each of four guns, with twenty-one 6in. howitzer batteries and fifteen mountain batteries.

Belgian

On 13 May 1913, in response to the worsening political climate in Europe, the Belgian Government decided that the Belgian Army was to be increased to a strength of 340,000. However when war broke out just under a year later the army was still only 120,500 strong, of whom 3,500 were armed paramilitary police or *gendarmes*. Critically the army lacked 2,300 officers. As a stop-gap some 65,000 over-age reservists were called up to serve in static fortress regiments while 46,000 members of the Civil Guard were tasked with rear-area security.

In 1914 the Belgian Army consisted of fourteen infantry regiments of the line, three regiments of light infantry, a Grenadier regiment, a regiment of Riflemen, a battalion of Rifle Cyclists, and one corps of the Gendarmerie. In the cavalry, two regiments of Guides, three of Mounted Riflemen, and five regiments of Lancers were available. The artillery contained three Field regiments, two Horse groups, and three fortress groups. The Engineers consisted of just one regiment.

The Field Army contained 120,500 regulars and 18,000 volunteers. This was divided into six large divisions, each comprising 25–32,000 men. The divisions contained two or three brigades; each brigade had two infantry regiments of three battalions each and one machine gun company. Divisional artillery consisted of three batteries. The cavalry regiments were Mounted Rifles or Lancers. An aviation section was also available to aid with reconnaissance. The army had also one Cavalry Division available, it contained two brigades, instead of the planned three.

Three months into the war the Belgian Army had suffered huge casualties in comparison to its small size having lost 9,000

8. Belgian and British troops fight alongside each other at Ypres. (The War Illustrated Album DeLuxe, Vol. 1, Amalgamated Press, London, 1915, Courtesy of the Great War Photo Achive: www.gwpda.org.uk)

killed, 15,000 wounded and several tens of thousands captured, missing or forced to flee into the neutral Netherlands and so into internment. The total available manpower had been reduced to 80,000 men. Of these, only 48,000 still carried their personal weapons. The little force was supported by 184 machine guns and 306 artillery pieces. However, in the fighting it had acquitted itself with honour and motor vehicle mounted machine gun crews had delayed German forces and in so doing demonstrated the lethal potential of combining the internal combustion engine with the machine gun – a combination that still works in 2011.

British

The British Army would be the weakest field force of the four combatants at the First Battle of Ypres. In Britain there was a popular story that comparing the British Expeditionary Force (BEF) in France with the mass conscription European armies, Kaiser Wilhelm of Germany had dismissed it as a 'contemptible little army'. It was probably an effective piece of recruiting propaganda by the British, but in essence it was not untrue.

The British saw their role as maintaining dominance of the seas, and offering financial support, whilst providing a small highly trained army to supplement the French. In equipment and resources the British Army – a career force of professionals took second place to the Royal Navy. Later in the war as recruits were put through their training, exasperated Non Commissioned Officers (NCOs) watching civilians struggling to become soldiers would utter 'Thank Gawd we've got a Navy'.

The role of the pre-war British Army was primarily policing the empire and units were deployed throughout Britain's imperial possessions, however this meant that often forces at home were understrength. Indeed, in echoes of current moves in the early twenty-first century, prior to the First World War, the army itself had been reduced by 16,000 men as a politically acceptable cost-cutting exercise. However, it was those understrength units stationed at home that were to form the basis of the expeditionary force (later known as the British Expeditionary Force (BEF)) that was to be sent to France in 1914. The force was initially made up of six formed infantry divisions and a cavalry division, which would be created from existing brigades on mobilisation. To bring these formations up to war strength 60 per cent of their manpower were reservists. After the outbreak of war, units serving abroad were brought home to form additional Regular divisions.

Alongside the Regular Army, there was the Territorial Force (TF) of fourteen infantry divisions and fourteen Yeomanry brigades. The Territorials, as part-time volunteers, were often viewed with some suspicion by the Regular Army, as many of them had not seen active service. The Territorial Force's primary role was home defence and its members could only be sent overseas if they volunteered and only a small number of units had done so before the outbreak of war, but this soon changed. During the early weeks of the war, the BEF was to suffer heavy casualties and so individual TF units began to be sent to France in September 1914 (at the same time three TF divisions were sent to replace Regular units overseas). The first TF division did not, however, deploy to an active theatre of war until March 1915. However, once in the frontline regular soldiers, though they were happy to

33

9. *In 1914 there was optimism and enthusiasm for war when men left for France. By the latter years, when the rush of volunteers had dried up and conscription had been introduced there was grim acceptance that the departure for the Western Front might be a one way trip.*

tease them, were more than happy to be reinforced by Territorial soldiers. Rifleman Henry Williamson of the London Rifle Brigade (a Territorial formation) recalled that at Ypres in 1914:

> We were brigaded with regulars who wore balaclava helmets. The whole feeling was one of tremendous comradeship, and

these old sweats who were survivors of Mons and the Aisne,
they had no fear at all, and any apprehension we had of going
in under fire was soon got rid of in the trenches.

from Max Arthur, *Forgotten Voices of the Great War*

However, Lord Kitchener, Secretary of State for War, unlike the
Germans, was prepared for a long war and realised that Britain
would need a large army to see out the conflict. He, too, did not
hold the Territorials in high regard and therefore decided to raise
a mass all-volunteer army (later dubbed Kitchener's Army), who
would receive similar training to that of Regular Army units. The
men of the New Armies, as they were called, enlisted for four
years or the duration of the war. Shortage of equipment and
facilities meant that it would be many months before any of these
new divisions deployed overseas.

In the early months of 1914 Corporal Clarke of the Gordon
Highlanders recalled that class still dominated the army and in
Ypres while the men slept on floors and in outhouses, the officers
slept in beds in the most affluent houses in the town:

The hell they were all about to enter was to virtually destroy
that differential; when men are at their Maker's door and flying
shrapnel can open that door at any minute of the day, every
day, there was to be a bond built up between the two.

from van Emden, *The Soldier's War*

Enthusiastic but untrained volunteers bolstered reserves, 51,647
enlisted in August 1914 and that figure rose to 174,901 by
5 September, just eight weeks prior to First Ypres. While some
4,192 of the regular soldiers had more than fifteen years of
experience, 46,291 had just under two years. The British Army
fielded just 4,000 gunners and seventy-six guns per division. Each
infantry battalion contained just two machine guns. The solitary
Cavalry Division was comprised of only 9,000 men, twenty-four
machine guns and the same number of light artillery pieces.

The British Soldier

Until the ranks were filled with volunteers who signed up for 'the duration of the war' – words that produced the catchphrase among soldiers 'roll on Duration', the British Expeditionary Force was composed of career soldiers. They were dedicated, loyal and very well trained – however, for the general public, the peacetime army was not seen as a prestigious career for men who served in the ranks. In elite cavalry and infantry regiments officers were drawn from titled and landed families; however, the Royal Engineers and Royal Artillery, which emphasised technical skill, attracted soldiers and officers of a more intellectual calibre.

The role of the British Army prior to the First World War had been to serve as an Imperial police force – backed by locally recruited regiments composed of British officered indigenous forces. Australia, South Africa, Canada and New Zealand had their own territorial forces and these would form the basis of the huge armies they deployed to the Western Front.

Wartime initiatives such as the creation of 'Pals Battalions' encouraged men to join up to fight alongside friends and colleagues. In some cases, entire villages of men went off to war together. This was to have a profound effect on society in Britain, when thousands of these men became the 'Lost Generation'.

10. A sergeant with his load carrying equipment, rifle and bayonet stowed in the training manual positions. In the frontline equipment might be discarded or modified to suit the conditions while officers would make private purchases of clothing, like the waterproof trench coat.

11. *The British 18 pounder deployed during an exercise in Britain. This versatile field gun had a range of 7,000 yards but with improved ammunition this was eventually raised to 11,000 yards by the end of the war.*

THE ACTION OF SHRAPNEL EXPLAINED IN DIAGRAM.

TIME FUSE SHRAPNEL.—The shell, fired from gun at right against entrenched infantry, bursts about 80 yards in front of the latter and about 15 feet above the ground. The short lines indicate the zone covered by the bullets.

PERCUSSION SHRAPNEL.—The shell, fired from gun at right against advancing infantry, bursts upon hitting the ground, throwing a shower of bullets at approaching men. It is also used against buildings, but is ineffective on soft ground.

CASE (SHRAPNEL) SHOT.—Used at short range against cavalry. The shell bursts immediately after leaving the gun. At 200 yards range the lateral spread is 25 yards.

12. *At the outbreak of the First World War, artillery was still seen as a close support direct fire weapon and so shrapnel and case shot would be used against infantry and cavalry. However, High Explosive (HE) would be essential to destroy trenches and bunkers.*

The British could say that what they lacked in quantity they made up for in quality. Their NCOs and soldiers were highly trained. As a result of their experiences in the war in South Africa, British infantry were very proficient marksmen, capable of firing twenty aimed rounds per minute – a rate that came to be known as 'the Mad Minute'.

The Royal Artillery also lagged behind the Germans and French in 1914. Guns were still expected to provide infantry with close support in the frontline and the technique of indirect fire was largely ignored. It was the superiority of rifle fire that was considered decisive. There were fifty-four field artillery guns and eighteen Howitzers per division. There was no corps-level artillery control, no reserves in case of heavy losses, very little doctrine and there were not the appropriate numbers of staff or communications for effective artillery–infantry cooperation. Possibly the greatest defect was the lack of a High Explosive (HE) shells. Those that the gunners did have were few in number and hampered by a defective fuse, a problem which would not be fully resolved until 1916. Ultimately, the lack of Treasury support meant that there was little the army could have done to rectify these problems before the war.

However, in the Mk I 18 pounder the British had an elegant and well-designed gun that would serve throughout the war. It had a range of 7,000 yards but this was upped to between 9 and 11,000 yards in improved versions. Such was the quality of the 18 pounder that it would eventually form the basis of the 25 pounder of the Second World War, which was eventually retired in the 1970s.

Canadian Expeditionary Force

The Canadian Expeditionary Force (CEF) was a largely volunteer force, with conscription only being introduced in January 1918. Ultimately, only 24,132 conscripts arrived in France before the end of the war. Its soldiers earned a formidable reputation as hard fighters on the Western Front, as did soldiers from Australia and New Zealand. The First World War would help forge their distinct sense of nationhood and national identity.

In 1914 Canada was the senior Dominion in the British Empire and automatically declared war with Germany upon the British declaration. Of the first contingent formed at Valcartier, Quebec in 1914 it was reported that 'fully two-thirds were men born in the United Kingdom'. By the end of the war in 1918, at least 50 per cent of the CEF consisted of British-born men. Recruiting was difficult among the French-Canadian population, although one battalion, the 22nd, popularly known as the 'Van Doos', a corruption of the French for twenty-two (*vingt-deux*) was a French-Canadian formation.

At its maximum strength the CEF consisted of 260 numbered infantry battalions and two named infantry battalions: The Royal Canadian Regiment and Princess Patricia's Canadian Light Infantry; thirteen Mounted Rifle regiments, thirteen railway troop battalions, five pioneer battalions, as well as numerous ancillary units including field and heavy artillery batteries, ambulance, medical, dental, forestry, labour, tunnelling, cyclist and service units.

A distinct entity within the CEF was the Canadian Machine Gun Corps. It consisted of several motor machine gun battalions, the Eatons, Yukon, and Borden Motor Machine Gun batteries, and nineteen machine gun companies. During the summer of 1918, these units were consolidated into four machine gun battalions, one being attached to each of the four divisions in the Canadian Corps.

The Commanders

Some of the officers who commanded forces at the First Battle of Ypres would remain at the salient – rising in rank and responsibility. For some it was the graveyard of their careers. A few were sacked but others were posted away to less challenging commands. The French Army had a slang word – *Limogé* – implying that the failed general had been posted to the city of Limoges far from the front where he would be given a titular command. As casualty rates mounted there were personality clashes at the highest level with officers angered

Albrecht Duke of Württemberg

Commander of the German Fourth Army at Ypres, Albrecht Duke of Württemberg was born in Vienna in 1865. He led his army at the Battle of the Marne and had then been transferred to Flanders. The men under his command, though highly motivated, were not as well trained as some of their contemporaries and consequently their performance in the field did not match up to their enthusiasm. This was demonstrated by the failure to follow up the first gas attack at Ypres that had left the front wide open.

Duke Albrecht was awarded Imperial Germany's highest military decoration, the Pour le Mérite, in August 1915. This elegant blue enamel cross was a neck decoration known affectionately as The Blue Max. Among the soldiers who won it during the First World War were Rommel and Herman Goering – theirs however were for gallantry in the field whereas Duke Albrecht's was for competence in command and was essentially political. He was already a holder of the Austrian Order of the Golden Fleece and the Military Merit Cross – the latter won at the beginning of the First World War. A year after he was awarded the Pour le Mérite, he was promoted to Field Marshal. The army group that he commanded in 1917 was named after him and was responsible for the quieter southern sector of the Western Front until the Armistice of 1918.

At the end of the war the abdication of the Kaiser led to a change in the fortunes of the German aristocracy and though he was the heir to the throne of Württemberg he never took the crown. He died in October 1939 – a month after the outbreak of the Second World War.

by what they saw as crass or ill-thought through plans and tactics. However the Ypres Salient would also be the proving ground for outstanding British commanders, men like Allenby and Rawlinson.

German

The German Fourth Army was commanded by 50-year-old Field Marshal Albrecht, Duke of Württemberg or Albrecht Herzog von Württemberg (Albrecht Maria Alexander Philipp Joseph von Württemberg, head of the Royal House of Württemberg). The Field Marshal would remain in command of the Fourth Army during the Second Battle of Ypres and nominally in command in Flanders until February 1917 when he was sent to Strasbourg, where his Army Group Herzog Albrecht successfully defended Alsace Lorraine until the end of the war.

The Fourth Army consisted of the III Reserve Corps commanded by General Hans Hartwig von Beseler and was made up of the 5th and 6th Reserve divisions and the 4th Ersatz Division. In the panoply of royal and aristocratic German commanders von Beseler was something of a maverick, for a start his father was a university professor. Von Beseler junior had fought with distinction in the Franco-Prussian War and been ennobled by the Kaiser. In 1914 von Beseler was recalled from retirement and was given command of the III Reserve Corps in the German First Army led by General Alexander von Kluck. The German Army took Brussels on 20 August, and with the capital city in their hands von Kluck considered that the Belgian Army had been defeated. The main force of the German armies marched toward France, leaving the III Reserve Corps behind. Beseler was ordered to take possession of the city of Antwerp on 9 September and the siege that ensued ended almost a month later. Following the fighting at Ypres, von Beseler became governor of Poland, where he was a humane and tolerant governor.

The XXII Reserve Corps, under Erich von Falkenhayn, contained the 43rd and 44th Reserve divisions. Von Falkenhayn was an able

13. Erich von Falkenhayn.

and shrewd commander who realised that Germany had not won a quick war on the Western Front and that consequently if it was to engage in a war of attrition it would have to be on Germany's terms. After being made chief of staff of the German Army, it was he who proposed an attack on the French city of Verdun in 1916 to ensure that the French suffered unacceptable losses in a battle where prestige overrode military logic.

Von Hügel commanded XXVI Reserve Corps, comprising 51st and 52nd Reserve divisions. General von Carlowitz, and later General von Schubert commanded XXVII Reserve Corps, containing the 53rd and 54th Reserve divisions.

The German Sixth Army was under the command of Rupprecht Crown Prince of Bavaria (Kronprinz Rupprecht von Bayern). To give him his full title he was His Royal Highness Rupprecht Maria Luitpold Ferdinand, Crown Prince of Bavaria, Duke of Bavaria, of Franconia and in Swabia, Count Palatine of the Rhine. More intriguingly in 1919 he would become the Jacobite heir to the thrones of England, Ireland, Scotland and France following the death of his mother. Photographs show what appears to be a typical aristocratic German officer; however, Rupprecht was not

Rupprecht Crown Prince of Bavaria

Born in Munich in 1869 the Commander of the German Sixth Army, Crown Prince Rupprecht combined a military and a legal career. He attended the war academy in 1889, rising through the ranks from regimental commander in 1899 to commander of the Bavarian I Army Corps in 1906, with the rank of general of the infantry. Bavaria had retained some independence after the unification of Germany, one feature of which was the possession of its own army. While his status as heir to the Bavarian throne helped him rise through the ranks, Prince Rupprecht took his military duties seriously and would prove to be a capable commander.

His professionalism and competence had been demonstrated early in the war. He was given command of the German Sixth Army sent to Lorraine to repel the anticipated French advance as set out in the pre-war Plan XVII that aimed to recapture territory lost in the Franco-Prussian War. In the Battle of Lorraine, which began on 14 August, Rupprecht's forces feigned retreat under the force of the French attack, but launched a counterattack after luring the French armies into a heavily defended position covered by machine guns and heavy artillery.

He commanded throughout the war on the Western Front up to the Ludendorff Offensive of 1918, which he feared would not succeed because he believed it would run out of impetus.

Crown Prince Rupprecht was the only one of the German royal generals who deserved to hold his high command during the war. He combined military ability with an understanding of the suffering of his troops, and towards the end of the war an appreciation that the war was being lost. His suggestion for a negotiated peace in June 1918 was perhaps Germany's best chance to salvage a partial victory by that stage in the fighting – even in October Allied leaders were concerned that a German peace offer combined with a last stand on German soil could have undermined the public will to fight on.

He died in 1955.

only a royal prince whose performance in the field showed that he merited the high command he held, but he was also a humane and realistic man. He was born in 1869 and died in 1955 seeing Germany go to war twice and suffer devastating defeats. In 1917 he argued that Germany would lose the war and asserted this again in 1943 making him unpopular with the Nazis who imprisoned his wife and children.

HITLER'S WAR

In the inter-war years as the Nazis fought for political power, Hitler was keen to portray himself as a straightforward soldier who had seen his share of fighting around Ypres and been decorated for his bravery as a runner carrying messages in the frontline. However, *Hitler's First War* by historian Thomas Weber has called into question this version of the Führer's military service. The regiment in which Hitler served, the 16th List Bavarian Reserve Infantry, was said to be made up of patriotic and passionate student volunteers – men who would later become ardent Nazis. Checking the regimental roll, it shows that in fact a very large number of the soldiers were Jewish. The regiment saw its share of fighting but Hitler was often away from the front and never as he writes in *Mein Kampf* was he in 'the midst of bombardment' and nor did he 'risk death everyday'. In late October 1914 at Gheluvelt, Hitler asserted that he was the only survivor in his platoon – however the regimental records show that on the day in question only thirteen men in his company were killed in action. His Iron Cross decorations were more of a commendation for a job well done as a runner than for a specific act of bravery. The 1930s version of Hitler's war record was a product of Nazi propaganda assisted by veterans of the regiment who published their own self-seeking accounts of the war in which Hitler's prowess was exaggerated.

The Armies

The Sixth Army contained II Corps composed of the 3rd and 4th Regular Infantry divisions commanded by General Alexander Adolf August Karl von Linsingen who is reckoned to be one of the best German field commanders during the First World War despite having not served on the general staff. Following the fighting on the Marne and First Ypres he was transferred to the Eastern Front where he took command of Army Group South (1915) defeating the Russians at the Battle of Stryi in 1915 and taking 60,000 Russian prisoners. The Eastern Front would be the making of his reputation and following the Bolshevik Revolution and the Treaty of Brest Litovsk he became governor of Berlin. VII Corps was made of the 13th and 14th divisions and was commanded by General Eberhard von Claer (later general of the infantry).

General Gustav Hermann Karl Max von Fabeck commanded XIII Corps composed of 25th Reserve Division and 26th Division. During the First Battle of Ypres, Fabeck took control of an ad hoc battlegroup (Kampfgruppe), Group Fabeck, containing XV Corps under Berthold von Deimling, which contained the 30th and 39th divisions and II Bavarian Corps under General Karl von Martini, comprising the reallocated 26th Division from XIII Corps, and the 3rd and 4th Bavarian divisions. General von Fabeck was sixty at the time of the First Battle of Ypres and was an officer of considerable ability – being awarded the Pour le Mérite for outstanding planning and successful operations during the campaigns of 1914–15. However the pressure of command took its toll and he died from natural causes at Partenkirchen on 16 December 1916.

Two further corps would play a part in the battle, the XIX 'Saxon' Corps (24th Division and 40th Division) under General Maximilian von Laffert and XIV Corps (26th Reserve Division and 6th Bavarian Reserve Division), under General von Loden. One of the wartime volunteers who joined 6th Bavarian Reserve Division, Infantry Regiment 16, and who would rise to the rank of corporal was a 25-year-old frustrated painter, a troubled young Austrian named Adolf Hitler.

An indication of the flexibility of the German staff system was the ability to form battlegroups as the tactical situation dictated – it was a skill that would serve the Germans well in the Second World War. Group Gerok comprised the 3rd and 25th Reserve divisions, 6th Bavarian Reserve Division and 11th Landwehr Brigade. Two further groups were also committed: XV Corps which had been taken from Fabeck's Kampfgruppe was transferred to Kampfgruppe Linsingen during the battle. Karl von Plettenberg's Corps, which bore his name, contained the 4th Division, seconded from II Corps, and a Guards Division.

The cavalry had four corps: I Cavalry Corps (Guards and 4th Cavalry Division), II Cavalry Corps (2nd and 7th Cavalry divisions), IV Cavalry Corps (6th and 9th Cavalry divisions), V Cavalry Corps (3rd Cavalry and Bavarian Cavalry divisions) under Generals von Richthofen, von der Marwitz, Lieutenant General von Hollen and General von Stetten respectively.

French

The French Army at Ypres contained the Détachement d'Armée de Belgique, commanded by General Victor Louis Lucien d'Urbal and consisting of the IX Corps composed of 16th and 7th Cavalry divisions, with the 7th and 18th Infantry divisions, under General Pierre Dubois; XVI Corps under General Paul François Grossetti composed of 31st, 32nd, 39th and 43rd Infantry divisions; XXXII Corps under General Georges Louis Humbert composed of 38th, 42nd, 89th Territorial and 4th Cavalry divisions as well as the Fusilier Marine Brigade; XX Corps under General Maurice Balfourier composed of 11th and 26th divisions; the I Cavalry Corps under General Conneau composed of 1st, 3rd and 10th Cavalry divisions, and General Antoine de Mitry's II Cavalry Corps composed of the 87th Territorial, 5th and 9th Cavalry divisions).

British

Sir John French was commander-in-chief of the British Expeditionary Force, overseeing: I, II, III, IV Corps, and the Cavalry and Indian Corps. He was a strong character, with a fiery temper, known for challenging both his superiors and subordinates.

General Douglas Haig commanded I Corps. Haig's reputation would suffer after his death – first at the pen of David Lloyd George, the wartime Prime Minister, who wrote his account in his 'War Memoirs', published after Haig's death that Haig was 'intellectually and temperamentally unequal to his task'. In the 1960s Alan Clark writing about Haig asserted that a German general had said that British soldiers were 'lions led by donkeys' – though he later admitted he invented the quote. In reality Haig was a highly educated man who, as the French Army collapsed in mutiny and the Russians evaporated into the Bolshevik Revolution, kept the British Army together and made it the war-winning machine that defeated Imperial Germany in 1918. Lloyd George's memoirs were largely designed to enhance his own reputation while concealing his own culpability, particularly in respect of refusing to believe intelligence warnings of a great German attack in early 1918 and starving the army of manpower at a critical stage of the war. With the release of official First World War records under the '50-year rule' military historians began to look at the war with a more informed view, principally driven by the work of the historian John Terraine.

I Corps contained the 1st Infantry Division under the command of Lieutenant General Samuel Lomax. Not long before the outbreak of war Lomax, then a 59-year-old major general, was told that his military career had run its course and he would soon be required to retire. War changed everything and Lomax was given command of 1st Division as part of the British Expeditionary Force under Sir John French. Lomax also led his division during the Battle of the Marne and the counterattack at the Aisne. His operations were so successful that it has been said that he was 'the best Divisional General of those early days of the war'. On 19 October, he received notice that he was to be promoted to lieutenant general and was in the frame to command a corps when one became available.

In October the 1st Division established its headquarters at Hooge Château to the east of Ypres. On 31 October Lomax held a conference at the château with Major General C.C. Monro commanding 2nd Division. The staff cars parked around the château were spotted by a German pilot, the position reported, and a battery fired three 5.9in. shells at the location. The first shell exploded in the garden and, showing their inexperience of the type of warfare, some of the officers moved to the window. The second shell burst almost immediately outside killing six officers and fatally wounding two others – one of whom was Lieutenant General Lomax. Monro was not among the dead and injured, having moved to another part of the château. Lomax was evacuated to London but died on 10 April 1915 and so became one of seventy-eight British and Dominion officers of the rank of brigadier general and above to be killed in action during the First World War.

The 2nd Infantry Division was commanded by Major General Charles Carmichael Monro. Monro was a veteran of the Second Boer War and was present at the Battle of Paardeberg in 1900. Following the First Battle of Ypres he was promoted General Officer Commanding (GOC) I Corps and then GOC Third Army before being appointed Commander-in-Chief (C-in-C) of the Mediterranean Expeditionary Force. Ironically it was not a victory, but a withdrawal that showed his skill as a planner and commander. Following the dismissal of the force commander General Sir Ian Hamilton, Monro took command of a difficult situation at Gallipoli on the Turkish coastline in October 1915. He ordered the withdrawal from the peninsula and through meticulous planning an operation that could have turned into a disaster was completed with surprisingly few losses. In 1916 Monro briefly commanded the British First Army in France before being posted to India as C-in-C India.

II Corps was commanded by General Horace Smith-Dorrien. The general who was known behind his back as 'SD' and because of a fiery temper 'Smithereens', was a very experienced veteran of numerous colonial wars. In August 1914 Smith-Dorrien had been given command of the Home Defence Army; however, following the sudden death of Sir James Grierson, Lord Kitchener gave him command of II Corps confident that he could stand up to Field Marshal Sir John French, commander of the BEF. French had favoured General Plumer for the command of II Corps.

II Corps bore the brunt of a heavy flanking assault by the German forces at Mons. French ordered a general retreat, during which I Corps commanded by General Douglas Haig and II Corps became separated and I Corps did not reach its intended position to the immediate east of Le Cateau. In what was a classic example of 'reading the battle' Smith-Dorrien, now at Le Cateau, realised that his isolated forces were in danger of being overwhelmed in a piecemeal fashion. So he concentrated his corps, supplemented by Allenby's cavalry and Thomas D'Oyly Snow's 4th Division, and on 26 August launched a vigorous defensive spoiling action, which despite heavy casualties, halted the German advance. With the BEF saved, he resumed an orderly retreat. His decision to stand and fight enraged French who accused Smith-Dorrien of jeopardising the whole BEF, an accusation which was not well received by Smith-Dorrien's fellow corps commander, Haig, who already believed French to be incompetent.

On 26 December 1914, Smith-Dorrien took command of the Second Army. It was following the first German gas attack in the Second Battle of Ypres that, on 27 April, Smith-Dorrien recommended withdrawal to a more defensible line around Ypres. French used what he called this 'pessimism' as an excuse to sack Smith-Dorrien on 6 May. His replacement, the highly competent General Herbert Plumer, then recommended a withdrawal almost identical to that proposed by Smith-Dorrien, which French accepted. After the war Smith-Dorrien was heavily involved in servicemen's charities and became one of the founders of what is now the Royal British Legion.

Plumer would command the British V Corps under Smith-Dorrien in the Second Battle of Ypres. Plumer is generally regarded as one of

Sir John French

John French, the son of Captain William French RN and Margaret Eccles, was born in Ripple, Kent in 1852. He joined the Royal Navy in 1866, but transferred to the army in 1874. He served with the 19th Hussars in the Sudan (1884–85) and was a cavalry commander in South Africa during the Boer War (1899–1901).

Appointed Chief of Staff of the British Army in 1911, French took command of the British Expeditionary Force in August 1914. Ironically, his sister, Charlotte Despard was a Suffragette, member of Sinn Fein and one of Britain's leading anti-war campaigners. He himself appears to have suffered from mood swings – becoming very pessimistic about the outcome of the war following the fighting at Mons. Lord Kitchener, Secretary of State for War, had to apply pressure in order to persuade him to commit troops to the Marne offensive. Later French became overly optimistic as fighting settled into trench warfare. French resigned in December 1915 and Sir Douglas Haig replaced him as leader of the BEF.

French, as commander of the British Home Forces, was responsible for dealing with the Easter Rising in 1916. He was rewarded with the post of Lord Lieutenant of Ireland (1918–21). He survived an attempted assassination by the IRA while in this post. French was granted £50,000 by the British government when he retired and honoured with the title First Earl of Ypres.

French died in 1925.

14. Field Marshal Sir John French (extreme left) watches troops who are going 'Up The Line'. At the time, French was portrayed in the British media as a steady and experienced commander, although in reality his moods swung from pessimism to optimism and he gave conflicting orders.

the finest army commanders serving in France during the First World War. Unlike many of his fellow commanders, he had come from a lowly county regiment, the York and Lancasters. He could see that barbed wire and machine guns had made cavalry obsolete and the idea of the 'breakthrough', with cavalry exploiting the opening and pushing into the open country beyond the frontline was unrealistic. Plumer was a very careful planner, who husbanded men's lives and consequently earned their respect and affection. It was under his direction that the Messines Ridge to the south of Ypres would be attacked in June 1917, following the explosion of nineteen mines.

In December 1915, French himself was removed by Kitchener, after controversial handling of the reserves at the Battle of Loos, and replaced by Douglas Haig as commander of the BEF. From the outset of the First World War, French had demonstrated that he was a poor choice as commander of the BEF. He appears to have been a manic depressive with moods swinging from deep pessimism to gross over-optimism. He was, moreover, reluctant to cooperate with the French – Britain's allies, and, as the dismissal of Smith-Dorrien demonstrates, he bore grudges. Haig, his successor, likened his character to that of a soda-water bottle in that he was all froth and bubble but lacked the ability to think clearly and come to a reasoned decision. It is perhaps ironic that French accepted the title First Earl of Ypres.

II Corps contained the 3rd Infantry Division commanded by General Hubert Hamilton and 5th Infantry Division under General Charles Fergusson. Fergusson's son, Bernard, would serve with distinction as a Chindit commander in Burma during the Second World War. Hamilton, known to his men as 'Hammy' was a popular and experienced officer.

During August and September 3rd Infantry Division had been almost continuously engaged, fighting at Mons and Le Cateau and along the lines of the River Marne. In exhausting combat, casualties were massive and Hamilton came close to death on 26 September when a shell landed but did not detonate just feet away from where he and two other generals were discussing operations.

During the Race to the Sea Hamilton's division was in the vanguard and was heavily engaged in the opening weeks of October. On 14 October, Hamilton and his staff were on the road to the village of La Couture near Béthune on the frontlines to observe the situation. They had just dismounted when a large shrapnel shell burst overhead. Incredibly the officers who accompanied him were unhurt but a single ball entered Hamilton's forehead, killing him instantly. He was buried in the churchyard at La Couture, against the church wall with Smith-Dorrien in attendance and a representative of each of the regiments in the division as an honour guard. The only light was provided by car headlamps, and shell fire occasionally forced the chaplain to pause in the service. Indeed, fighting was so close during the brief ceremony that German small arms fire occasionally hit the walls and nearby graves, although none of the mourners were hit. Smith-Dorrien concluded the service with the words: 'Indeed a true soldier's grave. God rest his soul'. Once the fighting had moved on, his body was exhumed and reburied at St Martin's Church in Cheriton, England.

III Corps under the command of Lieutenant General William Pulteney was composed of 4th Division under General Henry Fuller Maitland Wilson and 6th Infantry Division under General John Keir. Keir would fall out with his superior and be forced to retire in 1916. Whereas some of these officers, notably Allenby would serve with distinction and take on higher ranks and more challenging commands in the First World War, Pulteney, a veteran of the Second Boer War and the Anglo-Egyptian War, would remain in command of III Corps until February 1918, when he took over XXIII Corps, commanding it until April 1919. After the war he was part of the British Military Mission to Japan. He was not highly regarded as an officer, being described by one of his subordinates as 'the most completely ignorant general I served during the war'.

The Cavalry Corps contained the 1st Cavalry Division under General H. de Lisle and the 2nd under Hubert Gough, and was led by General Edmund Allenby. Hubert de la Poer Gough enjoyed a meteoric career (helped perhaps by his thrusting style and the fact he came from a family that had three VC holders) but would be held unjustly responsible for the failure of the Fifth Army to halt Operation Michael, the massive German offensive of March 1918, and this would lead to his dismissal.

Allenby who was nicknamed 'The Bull' was a contemporary of Haig's. Though some officers found him overbearing – hence the nickname – he was a well read and gifted officer, posted to Egypt he took command of the Egyptian Expeditionary Force composed of British and Commonwealth forces. His service in the Palestine campaign included the liberation of Jerusalem from Turkish occupation on 9 December 1917. T.E. Lawrence the British officer who was the driving force behind the Arab Revolt that assisted Allenby's operations said of him: '[He was] physically large and confident, and morally so great that the comprehension of our littleness came slow to him'. Unlike the Western Front, Palestine was an ideal theatre for mobile warfare involving vehicles, and horse and camel mounted troops. Allenby's tactical skill in which he employed aircraft in a ground attack role along with these mobile forces was seen as the model for the Blitzkrieg warfare adopted by the Germans in the opening years of the Second World War.

IV Corps was commanded by General Henry Rawlinson, who in 1915 was promoted to the command of the British First Army. However, when he questioned the tactics being employed on the Western Front he was assigned to Gallipoli and given the 'poison chalice' of organising the withdrawal, alongside Monro. With sound planning and good leadership the evacuation went much better than was expected and would later be studied in Army Staff Colleges after the war. Rawlinson was recalled to the Western Front to assume command of the Fourth Army on 24 January 1916 as the plans for the Allied offensive on the Somme were being developed. On the night of 14 July men under his command launched the first large-scale night attack during the Battle of Bazentin on the Somme. A proponent of 'bite and hold' tactics he was known to the army as 'Rawly the Fox'. For a period in 1917–18, in addition to the Fourth Army, this talented and innovative officer also commanded the Second Army. He returned to the Fourth Army in July 1918 for the Allied counter-offensive. In this final offensive he combined ground attack aircraft with armour.

IV Corps was initially formed with the 7th Division, under Thompson Capper, and 3rd Cavalry Division commanded by Julian Byng. The 8th Division, intended to complete the corps, was still forming in England and did not arrive in France until 7 November, just before the First Battle of Ypres had ended.

7th Division was a wartime formation composed of three Regular Army battalions from Britain, together with nine battalions brought back from overseas stations. Formed at Chatham between 31 August and 4 October 1914, the division reached Zeebrugge on 6 October as part of the Antwerp Expedition, and only transferred to BEF control on 9 October, on formation of IV Corps. Byng's 3rd Cavalry Division had arrived in Belgium with only two of its three brigades, the third being formed at Zeebrugge after the division landed in the first week of October; it had only twelve field artillery pieces.

However the weakest formations were in James Wilcock's Indian Corps composed of 3rd Lahore Division under H.B.B. Watkis and 7th Meerut Division under C.A. Anderson. This formation had arrived in France at the end of September 1914.

The Soldiers

From the perspective of the early twenty-first century – almost 100 years after the First World War it can be hard to comprehend the background, motives and character of soldiers in the Great War.

In Britain, the Edwardian period that preceded the outbreak of the First World War was one of stability and a clearly defined social hierarchy, and this was reflected in the character of the national armed forces.

The Territorial Force, which would fill the gap left after the destruction of the BEF and its army of career soldiers, reflected the society from which it was drawn, with officers from the

15. Preserved German trenches at Bayernwald, the use of hurdles to revet the trench walls was a typically German technique. The advantage was that hurdles were light and easy to transport and were made from non-strategic materials.

squirearchy or management and soldiers from the manual labourers or factory staff. One Territorial Force (TF) formation, The Civil Service Rifles, was formed largely from the ranks of the Civil Service and The Post Office Rifles was likewise composed of Post Office employees. It is easy to understand why career officers and soldiers in the British Regular Army viewed the TF with a mixture of suspicion and contempt – however it was a Territorial formation that would hold Ypres at the outset of the fighting and one pre-war TF soldier William 'Bill' Slim would rise to the rank of Field Marshal in the Second World War and command the Fourteenth Army in Burma.

Social cohesion and lack of mobility meant that county and city loyalties were very strong. The volunteer Kitchener armies drew on this, forming Pals, Sportsmen's or Public School battalions. Men went to war with their mates and often with their manager and foreman as company commander and company sergeant major. Whereas, in Germany and France officers were career soldiers who had sometimes begun their military training as school age cadets. Soldiers saw themselves as something of an elite dividing German society into two classes 'soldiers and swine'. While the French Army had its quota of aristocrats it was a more democratic force than that of Imperial Germany which had royal and titled officers. Soldiers in both armies were conscripts and could therefore include a cross-section of society, including well educated and mature men as well as simple peasants or industrial labourers.

Two things were true of almost all these soldiers. Many had deep-seated religious convictions. If you had lived a good life, repented on your death bed for sins committed and received absolution from a padre, you were destined for a happy afterlife. The trenches would test the men's faith to the limits and many would find that it would fail under the terrible strain. Closely linked to religion was patriotism – French, British or German soldiers believed in the right of the cause for which they were fighting and were proud to be citizens and soldiers of their mother or fatherland.

This led to a curious exchange on Christmas Day 1914 when British and German soldiers emerged from their trenches to mingle in no man's land. A British officer observed the words '*Got Mit Uns*' on the belt buckle of a German soldier and asked what it meant. The English-speaking German officer confidently replied 'God with Us'. 'Oh no', came the equally confident reply, 'He's with us'. The British soldiers couldn't resist punning the motto, explaining to their German counterparts that they were quite happy and their hands were warm because they had 'Got mittens'.

The other feature that marks out the soldiers or 'Tommies' of the First World War is that they often came from very tough backgrounds. The lives of those drawn from the great cities were marked by overcrowding, poor sanitation and poor diet. Those from the country fared little better with agricultural labourers earning little and often dependant on their employers for housing. They entered the army with no great expectations and indeed before the war it was not the first choice of many young men.

However, men who had volunteered after 1914 and even those who had been conscripted changed during basic training – a regime of good food, exercise and discipline saw them build up muscle and become fitter and stronger. In barracks many had access to decent sanitation for the first time and with it enjoyed improved health. However their grim urban or rural childhoods and youth would be something of a preparation for life in the trenches. Lice and other pests and vermin were not a novelty to the rank and file – to officers the first encounter must have been repellent. In quiet times at the front men would kill off the eggs laid by the lice in the seams and folds of clothing – one method was to run the flame of a candle over the area. Since lice were known colloquially as 'chats' a group of men sat around talking and de-lousing their clothing were 'chatting'.

Even men from these hard backgrounds could be ground down by the stress of combat. Soldiers today would recognise what Lieutenant Colonel C.K. Burnett, the commanding officer of the 18th (Queen Mary's Own) Hussars saw in the faces of infantry at Ypres in 1914:

> We... noticed how weary the infantry was with its incessant fighting, the men seemed to have that faraway look on their faces which betokened general inability to realise the horrors which were surrounding them... the war had left them now with just a fixed determination to go on until they dropped, without notice of other events beyond what occurred in just their immediate front; one could too plainly see that the limit of human endurance had almost been reached.

Men broke and the punishment for military crimes was severe. The military penal code had grown to deal with an army drawn, as the Duke of Wellington observed a mere century before the First World War, from the 'scum of the earth'. It was a harsh code and reflecting the fact that the breaking of military law could mean death or disaster for one's comrades. Cowardice, casting away of arms in the face of the enemy, striking an officer and desertion were all punishable by death. The punishment for murder in civil courts was death by hanging; the army executed soldiers in wartime by firing squad. These executions, the majority of them for desertion, were almost exactly 10 per cent of those actually condemned; of the just over 3,000 soldiers condemned to death between August 1914 and March 1920 the vast majority had their sentences commuted to hard labour or penal servitude. In most cases of those actually executed it was for a second or third offence. At least half of the of the 306 men executed for military offences by the British Army during the First World War were serving in the Ypres Salient. Today some of these men would be treated as psychological casualties, suffering from post-traumatic stress disorder, some however were guilty of criminal acts and it is a luxury to judge the conduct of the past from the secure standpoint of today. In the grim league of death by execution in the First World War, France and Italy executed the largest number at about 600 each, while New Zealand executed five. These numbers should be regarded in the context of the many millions who served, of which they make a sad, but minuscule, number. Tragic as some of these deaths may have been, after the war the British authorities still recorded the names of those executed on memorials such as the Menin Gate.

For lesser crimes there were a range of Field Punishments. If a soldier was sentenced to Number 1 he was tied to a wagon wheel spread-eagled with the hub in his back, and his ankles and wrists secured to the rim. Private W. Underwood of the 1st Canadian Division was given seven days Number 1 – he did 'two hours up and four hours down for seven days, day and night'. And, he recalled years later 'the cold! It was January 1915… And the only reason I was there was because I missed a roll-call'. Old soldiers regarded Field Punishment Number 1 as a mild inconvenience. Frank Richards of the Regular 2nd Battalion Royal Welsh Fusiliers recalled that, while out of the line at Houplines, fifty-eight soldiers undergoing Field Punishment Number 1 were tied to railings when not doing fatigues. They did not mind the punishment but were outraged that French civilians could see them.

One of the ironies of trench warfare was that as it developed, frontline soldiers often felt a greater bond with the enemy a few hundred yards across no man's land, than they did with the civilians and politicians at home with their ranting and angry patriotism. In 1915 Sergeant John Grahl of 1st Battalion Highland Light Infantry recalled a German shouting 'Hang on until October and you can have the damned war', the British would shout back 'Come on over, Fritz you **** ***' or 'Gott strafe the Kaiser!' to which the reply came 'strafe the King!'. A policy of live and let live often developed and moving fresh troops into the line prior to an offensive was in part to ensure that the attack was pressed home with aggression and drive.

The Kit

The British Expeditionary Force that went to war in 1914 was arguably the best equipped and trained force in Europe. The khaki serge uniforms adopted in 1902 and worn by officers and men were the first real example of camouflaged combat clothing. Men wore a soft peaked cap with the regimental cap badge; officer's headgear from London hatters was of a superior quality.

Only the British had adopted webbing load carrying equipment in 1908 and this consisted of a wide belt, left and right ammunition pouches which held seventy-five rounds each, left and right braces, a bayonet frog (leather sheath) and attachment for the entrenching tool handle, an entrenching tool head in web cover, water bottle carrier, small haversack and large pack. A mess tin inside a khaki cloth cover was worn attached to one of the packs. Inside the haversack were personal items, knife and when on Active Service, unused portions of the daily ration. Some personal kit was carried in the large pack but was normally kept for carrying the soldier's greatcoat and or a blanket – in the field the greatcoat or blanket would be used as bedding at night. The full set of 1908 webbing could weigh over 70lb (32kg), however the equipment was well designed and the weight evenly

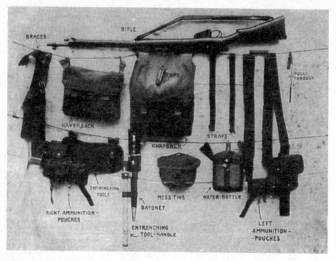

16. A soldier's equipment – the rifle is a Lee Metford – it was still in use with Territorial Force soldiers at the beginning of the war. If the webbing kit was properly adjusted the weight was well distributed over the waist and shoulders.

distributed. Due to manufacturing problems, however, pattern '08 webbing could not be produced in the quantity required. The volunteers of Kitchener's Army had to make do with leather equipment for load carrying.

In 1915 Fusilier Victor Packer of the Royal Irish Fusiliers recalled bitterly that a battalion coming out of the line at Ypres could march up to 12 miles (20km) to a base camp:

> You still had in those days, a full pack, 250 rounds of ammunition, water bottle, haversack, rifle, bayonet, and often you carried a bit of something extra as well. We were daft enough to carry souvenirs in those days like nose caps of shells and things or a Uhlan's helmet, whatever we could get like that we prized, but not long afterwards we threw them over a hedge or somewhere.
>
> from *Forgotten Voices of the Great War*

The Imperial German Army *feldgrau* – field grey serge uniform was also an effective neutral colour. German soldiers had leather load carrying equipment with a large pack constructed from cow hide with the fur retained on the outside flap to give extra waterproofing. Like all the combatants the Germans later adopted a steel helmet to replace the distinctive spiked helmets – head gear that was much prized as a trophy by British soldiers.

Incredibly the French went to war in uniforms that would have been better suited to the Napoleonic Wars – blue tunics and even red trousers and kepis (the distinctive French headgear). Officers armed with pistol and sword went into action in white gloves. Later in the war the French would adopt a blue-grey uniform known as horizon blue – the theory being that a man standing against the sky in a blue uniform would be harder to spot. Like the Germans they retained leather load carrying equipment, but followed the British practice of wearing short ankle boots with cloth puttees wrapped around the calf to give support and keep out dirt and small stones.

Weaponry

By 1914 all European armies had a magazine-fed bolt action rifle. The British Army had the Short Magazine Lee Enfield Mk III Rifle more commonly known as the SMLE; it was the standard infantry rifle in the First World War and would be for much of the Second World War. A bolt action weapon that fired a .303 calibre round it weighed 8.62lbs was 44½in. long and had a ten-round magazine. Sights were set out to 2,000 yards. The 'sword' bayonet fitted to the SMLE had a formidable 17in. blade; the theory behind this was that it gave a foot soldier sufficient reach to be able to bayonet a mounted soldier. A soldier could actually load eleven rounds if he had one in the breach, or 'up the spout', and this gave him a significant advantage over German soldiers whose Gewehr '98 had a five-round magazine. In the hands of a trained soldier the British Short Magazine Lee Enfield was easily capable of 15rpm

17. The Short Magazine Lee Enfield in the capable hands of a Rifleman who is demonstrating the correct way in which to load a charger (clip) of five rounds. The magazine held ten rounds and an eleventh could be loaded into the breach.

(rounds per minute) of accurate fire. However in the 1930s, a Small Arms School Corps Warrant Officer managed a rate of 37rpm. Reliable and extremely accurate, the SMLE is regarded by most authorities as the finest rifle of the First World War.

The 7.92mm Gewehr '98 introduced into service with the Imperial German Army on 5 April 1898 was designed by Paul Mauser and was the standard infantry weapon in the First World War. While the Mauser's action is superb and there are an estimated 102 million rifles with the model '98 bolt action worldwide, the rifle suffered, as we have seen, from its inferior magazine. However, the Mauser fired one of the highest velocity rounds of the First World War – the 'S round' had a muzzle velocity of 2,882ft per second (fps). In contrast the British .303 round exited the barrel at 2,060fps and the French rounds at 2,060fps. Higher muzzle velocity meant that a soldier could engage distant targets without having to make ballistic adjustments. In other words to hit a target at 700 yards a Lee Enfield round would climb to a height of 10ft from the ground, while a Mauser 'S round' reached approximately 6ft.

The 8mm Lebel Fusil Modèle 1886 with which the French Army entered the war had been the first service rifle to fire smokeless ammunition, although this was its only design distinction. It retained the straight bolt action of the Gras rifle of 1874. The French rifle was modified in 1893 and again five years later, but had one key fault. This was its eight-round tubular magazine derived from the Austrian Kropatschek rifle in which the bullet of one round butted up against the percussion cap of the cartridge case in front. It was slow to load and there was always the risk if the job was rushed that the bullet of one round would hit the percussion cap of the round in front and cause an explosion. The Lebel was replaced during the war by the 1907 Berthier; a more modern design that used the Berthier bolt action and the box magazine feed from the Mannlicher. The box was better than the tube magazine, but French soldiers were equipped with three-round clips in contrast to the five-round clips used by the British and Germans. The rifle was further modified in 1916 to take a five-round box magazine and the resulting weapon was widely used by a number of foreign armies in the inter-war periods.

Officers were armed with a revolver and sword – both were soon discarded since they made the user an obvious target for snipers.

The pistol carried by British officers was often the powerful British Webley .455 revolver, developed by Webley & Son (Webley & Scott Co. since 1897) in the 1870s. The British Webleys were the first top break revolvers with a two piece frame, which hinges (or breaks) at the forward low end for ejection and loading. The ejector operates automatically when the frame is broken open and all six empty cases are ejected simultaneously from the cylinder. The cartridges then can be inserted by hand. Designers of revolvers in all calibres adopted the top break system, as it made for quick reloading – crucial in a short-range fire fight. Webleys that had been rechambered for the .45 ACP (Automatic Colt Pistol) round had two three-round half-moon clips that further sped up reloading. The first Webley revolver was officially adopted for service in the British Army and Royal Navy in 1887, as a Webley Revolver .455 Mark I. It was a top break, six shoot, double action revolver, chambered for the .455 British Service cartridge. This cartridge fired a big 265-grain lead bullet, but because it used black powder it had a relatively slow muzzle velocity of 600fps. A smokeless version of this cartridge was later developed but this still had a low velocity since it could also be fired in early revolvers. All Webley revolvers were single/double action or double action only, with a very distinctive barrel shape and frame lock with lock lever on the left side of the frame and V-shaped lock spring on the right side.

A few years later, the French Army adopted an 8mm revolver the Modele D'Ordonnance (Lebel) 1892 – it was a revolver that would soldier on almost into the twenty-first century and particularly enjoyed a remarkable longevity in service with the French Army. The pistol had a conventional swing out cylinder with the release button on the right, which made it a user-friendly weapon for left-handed shooters. The revolver has an ingenious system that allows the left-hand side plate to swing forward on a hinge to expose the mechanism for cleaning. Like many weapons developed in the late nineteenth century the revolver used its own special 8mm ammunition. Though this was a robust and workmanlike weapon many French officers purchased their own self-loading pistols which their regarded as more chic – however this move would have presented ammunition supply problems.

However, the iconic pistol of the First World War and a much sought after trophy was the Luger self-loading pistol, known in German Army service as the Pistole 08 from its year of adoption. It was named after George Luger, a designer at the Ludwig Löwe small-arms factory in Berlin. The Lugers' design is based on earlier Hugo Borchard idea, but Luger re-designed the Borchard's locking system into a much smaller package. The first military Lugers were made in 1900 to a Swiss order. The original calibre was 7.65mm but in 1902 the firm of DWM, along with Luger, by request of the German Navy developed a new round, 9x19mm Luger/Para[bellum], one of the most common pistol cartridges in the world, by re-necking the case of the 7.65mm Luger round and the type was adopted for the German Navy in 1904. The standard pistol had an eight-round box magazine and fired a 9mm Parabellum round with a maximum effective range of 230ft. The toggle-joint mechanism was complex, but made the weapon comfortable to fire and therefore more accurate.

The pistol had its place in the quick and violent fighting patrols called 'trench raids' in which soldiers carried clubs, knuckle dusters and knives that were silent and could be used in trenches in hand-to-hand combat. Only the revolver or self-loading pistol was a useful weapon in these confined spaces. However, the First World War battleground would in many ways be dominated by the machine gun.

The Vickers .303 Medium Machine Gun Mk I entered service in 1912 and soldiered on with the British Army until 1974. It was a Maxim mechanism that had been inverted and improved. With water in the cooling jacket the gun weighed 40lb and the tripod 48.5lb – the total weight was 88.5lb. The Vickers machine gun had a muzzle velocity of 2,440fps, a rate of fire of 450 to 500rpm and fired from a 250-round fabric belt. After the war the introduction of the Mark VIII round added a further 1,000 yards to the 3,600yd maximum range. Using a dial sight that was introduced in 1942 the gun could be used for indirect fire. Its greatest drawback was that the massive weight of fire it delivered was only arrived at with the expenditure of huge amounts of ammunition. Added to this it required considerable amounts of water to keep it cooled during prolonged firing. Ideal in trench warfare where positions remained relatively static for months or even years, it was less useful in manoeuvre warfare where its weight and the problem of keeping it supplied with ammunition became problematic. During the First World War it gained a reputation as the 'Queen of the battlefield' particularly when employed by men of the British Machine Gun Corps that had been founded in October 1915. It is a measure of the effectiveness and reliability of the weapon that during the British attack upon High Wood on 24 August 1916 at the Battle of the Somme it is estimated that ten Vickers fired in excess of 1 million rounds over a 12-hour period.

The opposite number to the Vickers machine gun, the German Maschinengewehr 08 (MG08), was almost a direct copy of the 1884 Maxim Gun and the German Army's standard machine gun in the First World War. It was produced with a number of variations during the war. The MG08 remained in service until the outbreak of the Second World War in static positions; it was replaced by the MG34. It was withdrawn from frontline service by 1942. The 7.92mm MG08, based on the 1901 model but named after 1908 – its year of adoption, was water cooled by about one gallon of water in a jacket around the barrel. It fired from a 250-round fabric belt and had a cyclic rate of 400rpm, although sustained firing would lead to overheating. The MG08, like the Maxim Gun, operated on the basis of a toggle lock; once cocked and fired it would continue firing rounds until the trigger was released. Its practical range was estimated at some 2,200 yards up to an extreme range of 4,000 yards.

The French Army's standard heavy tripod mounted medium machine gun throughout the First World War was the Hotchkiss 8mm M1914 machine gun. Although it was reliable it was also unquestionably heavy at 50lb (23kg) (88lb (40kg) with its mounting). Initially adopted in 1900 a number of models were produced until a gas-operated, air-cooled model was produced in 1914. Although the gun was generally well regarded the Hotchkiss' twenty-four or thirty-round metal magazine strip, which fired 8mm Lebel rounds, was considered a notable design flaw. This was corrected when a 249-cartridge belt was introduced in 1915. The gun was still in service in the Second World War and captured weapons were used by the Germans in fixed fortifications on the Atlantic Wall. Even with the increased belt the gun was unable (for obvious reasons) to meet the theoretical cyclic rate of 600rpm, the practical firing capacity being 400rpm. The gun's maximum effective range was approximately 4,000 yards.

All infantry rifles were equipped with a bayonet – tracing its origins back to the pike it was said that the bayonet took its name from the French town of Bayonne. There were three basic designs in service in the First World War. The 'needle' bayonet mounted on the French Lebel rifle that was prone to breaking, the knife-bladed or sword bayonet found on the SMLE and Gewehr '98, and the serrated-edged pioneer version used by German combat engineers. The serrated edge made it an effective saw, however since it was said to produce a ragged wound it was held up by the Allies as an example of 'Hun frightfulness'. Bayonets were used in anger, however many men surrendered simply at the sight of a bayonet. They did have other uses and one British veteran said that they were used primarily for toasting food, poking a brazier, opening ration tins, and scraping mud off clothing, boots and rations. A candle could be secured to the grip with molten wax and the bayonet became an effective candlestick. Bayonets were sometimes ground down and modified as trench knives, with a shorter blade these were handy weapons in the confined space of a trench when a night-time raiding party needed to kill a sentry quickly and quietly.

The Tactics

The British had learned hard lessons in the Boer War at the turn of the nineteenth and twentieth centuries. The Boers were natural riders, hunters and marksmen equipped with excellent German Mauser rifles that fired smokeless ammunition. The British soldiers who had fought ill-armed native armies in colonial wars suffered heavy casualties until they learned the lessons of camouflage, field craft and marksmanship. The British Expeditionary Force that went to France in 1914 brought these formidable skills to bear against the German Army at Mons and their accurate and rapid fire from their excellent SMLE rifles did much to slow the German advance.

Britain declared war on 4 August 1914 and when by mid-August the Belgians had been mauled by the German Army only one intact force stood in their way – the British Expeditionary Force. The BEF fired its first shots of the war on 22 August. Next day the advancing German infantry were pulled up short near Mons as the withering rifle fire of the British caused them heavy casualties, two days later at Le Cateau the story of Mons was repeated, only on a bloodier scale. Once again the Germans attacked in tightly bunched waves and again they were met with rifle fire so intense that they thought the British were equipped with machine guns.

Tactics changed during the war and what might now be called SOPs – Standard Operating Procedures had emerged by the end of the conflict. At the beginning of the war the French particularly were keen to press the attack. In part this was a philosophical concept based on the desire to regain the territory lost in the Franco-Prussian War. The French theorist Colonel C.J.J. Ardent du Picq believed that morale was the winning factor while Marshal Ferdinand Foch expressed the belief that it was impossible to lose a battle until the general believed himself defeated. In 1914 even though the first trench warfare had been fought in the Russo-Japanese War and even in parts of the American Civil War, few

18. A British officer inspects a Lewis Light Machine Gun on a 'Louch Pole' mounting in a frontline trench. The picture was taken after the Mk I steel helmet had been introduced.

theorists imagined it would happen in Europe where a conflict would surely be one of manoeuvre.

In 1914 a German Army battalion had six Maxim MG Model 1908 machine guns, while in contrast a British battalion initially had only two Vickers Mk Is or Maxims. However, from the outset of the fighting the Germans tactically concentrated these already coordinated battalion teams into batteries and thus gave the appearance, and effect, of having even more machine guns than they actually did. This appeared the case at Loos when German machine gun crews opened fire at 1,400 metres on the advancing British infantry on the afternoon of 26 September 1915. They inflicted 8,000 casualties (50 per cent) on just two British New Army divisions (21st and 24th). One single German machine gun crew is said to have fired 12,500 rounds.

GRENADES

Following their use in the Russo-Japanese War at the beginning of the twentieth century, a commission from the Imperial German Army had examined the lessons and as a result the Germans went to war in 1914 armed with reliable hand grenades.

The first German models consisted of a serrated sphere about 2.9in. (76mm) in diameter filled with gunpowder, with a friction-activated fuse at the top and a ring pull.

This grenade was followed by the *Stiehlhandgranate* ('Stick Grenade') and the *Eierhandgranate* – an egg-shaped grenade. The latter was 10.5oz (0.3kg) and the former 1.5lb (0.7kg) – the egg grenade could be thrown 148ft (45 metres) and the stick under 98.4ft (30 metres). The explosive filler for both grenades was a mixture of gunpowder, potassium chlorate, barium nitrate and aluminium powder.

As fighting settled into trench warfare the value of the grenade became obvious and the French and British began by improvising devices. Some were made from empty jam tins packed with explosives and nails, and fitted with a short length of safety fuse and a detonator – the thrower normally lit the fuse with a cigarette.

In the First Battle of Ypres Captain Reginald Thomas of the Royal Artillery recalled how he teamed up with Sapper Captain Phillip Neame to produce these early IEDs 'made out of empty jam tins which were filled with rivets, hobnails and any small bits of metal'. They were crude but effective and as Thomas said 'you could throw them twenty or thirty yards. You couldn't have a nicer missile to hurl. We did rather well with them'.

The British and French munitions industry eventually caught up with the Germans and the French standardised with the VB or Viven-Bessieres grenade and the British with the Mills Bomb, or No. 5 grenade.

The Mills Bomb – named after its designer and inventor William Mills would enter service with the British Army in 1915 and with minor modifications soldier on into the late 1970s as the No. 36 grenade.

In 1917–18 the British and Germans made a change from a defensive to a more offensive role for the machine gun. The British had established the Machine Gun Corps to undertake highly coordinated offensive and defensive tactics, including barrages. The infantry then concentrated on the deployment, with much success, of the lighter Lewis machine guns at the platoon level. In many ways the infantry platoon in the latter part of the First World War with its specialist 'bombers' – men carrying bags of grenades, Lewis gunners providing fire for the riflemen and bombers to manoeuvre would be familiar to a platoon commander on operations in Afghanistan.

As early as 1914 Erwin Rommel, who would gain fame as the commander of the Afrika Korps in the Second World War, noted in his training manual 'Infantry Attacks' that though his platoon was under heavy fire from French positions they broke down into small groups and advanced in rushes. In what reads like current infantry tactics each group provided covering fire for the other. When they reached the French position the enemy had fled and the Germans realised that the reason their casualties were so low was that the French had not adjusted the sights on their rifles and were aiming high.

As can be imagined Rommel was the exception in 1914. At the time the British, French and Germans all believed that offence was the war-winning tactic and if supporting fire was concentrated correctly the impetus of the assault would succeed. The British 1914 manual 'Infantry Training' stated that casualties decreased with a steady advance because of the morale effect upon the enemy; in other words his fire would become erratic as he began to panic at the sight of his enemy closing with the position and because the range would be changing.

The tactics favoured by Rommel worked only if the platoon or company had good junior NCOs who could 'read the battle' and lead or drive the men under their command. Men like this could be rare in mass conscript armies, such as that at the beginning of the First World War, and consequently attacks were often made

19. A painting of Corporal Gibbons of the Royal Engineers constructing jam tin bombs in a frontline position. This was a hazardous business, but with factory-made grenades non existent or in short supply it was vital work at First Ypres.

by mass formations which when they came under small arms fire, one British soldier recalled, resembled 'a swaying football crowd'.

Terrain could shape the theory and practice of tactical formations. Edmund Priestman of the 6th Battalion, York and Lancaster Regiment described how in training his platoon adopted 'artillery formation' for advance across country. In this formation the platoon formed a loose column four abreast to (in theory) present the minimum target for artillery:

> Across the first field we kept this formation beautifully. Then we met a second hedge and then a wet ploughed field. On switching my attention from the ground to the platoon in front I found (by some unexplained means) they had disappeared and left no sign of themselves! At this point a head poked over a hedge and saw me – and wanted to know 'What the **** I thought I was doing?' To which I replied that 'I was under the impression that I was advancing in artillery formation'. On closer examination I found my formation was more like a Mothers' Meeting out for a walk... the Colonel (for the head belonged to no less!) cursed me and my Mothers' Meeting most vilely for ten minutes and then went in search of the Major to repeat the best bits over again to him...
>
> from Haythornthwaite, *The World War One Source Book*

Priestman's experience of the failure of command and control was in training; on the Western Front, shell and small arms fire would be the lethal addition to the mud, craters and barbed wire.

Barbed wire, which had been invented in 1867 in the United States, was first used as an obstacle in the Spanish-American War during the siege of Santiago and extensively in the Boer War, where it played a strategic role in bringing areas under control, at military outposts and also in holding the captured Boer population. At the turn of the century it was used in the Russo-Japanese War, a conflict that was almost a proving ground for weapons, tactics and equipment used in the First World War. Military barbed wire had longer barbs than agricultural wire and these were placed closer together than a hand's width. While it was thought that artillery fire could cut wire for localised breaching a more reliable system was the Bangalore torpedo, which was first devised in 1912 by Captain McClintock of the Madras Sappers and Miners, part of the British Indian Army and based at the military depot at Bangalore, India. The Bangalore torpedo consists of interlocking explosive filled tubes that can be pushed into a barbed wire belt. When it explodes shards of metal cut the wire while the blast pushes it to either side. A soldier can crawl forward and slide a Bangalore torpedo into place without enemy troops being aware that an attack is about to be launched. Wire cutters were the other way of breaching wire. Though they were heavy and rather cumbersome they could be issued widely and consequently gave soldiers their own individual breaching kit.

The commanders and soldiers at Ypres were to face all of these problems during the year 1914–15: coordination of artillery fire and infantry, the difficulties of overcoming terrain and barbed wire, as well as the horrors of chemical warfare – the German tactic that caused such devastation during the Second Battle of Ypres. The experience of all these elements which culminated in the realisation that the days of offensive warfare and full-on assaults with rapid movement were gone, to be replaced by a draining and demoralising existence of static and entrenched warfare that would characterise the Western Front.

THE DAYS
BEFORE BATTLE

The days before the First and Second Battle of Ypres differed greatly. First Ypres was characterised by manoeuvre and 'the fog of war'. For commanders to build up a clear intelligence picture in what was a rapidly changing situation was extremely difficult. Aircraft were available but they were not sophisticated machines – and the combination of pilot and observer in many of them was to ensure that one of the crew could give complete attention to spotting enemy troop movements, batteries or positions. The pilot often needed his full attention to keep the aircraft flying. Tethered observation balloons were also used and here a field telephone link meant that information could be passed rapidly to headquarters and their staff.

Radio communications were a very recent development, and as such they were cumbersome and unreliable. The First World War would see huge improvements in size and reliability, however communications would still rely on techniques that dated from the nineteenth century. Runners at company and battalion level would carry messages – crossing terrain in which there were few obvious reference points and sometimes doing this at night or in harsh weather was testing even for the fittest soldier.

Flags, heliography or pyrotechnics could be a fast, if obvious, way of signalling and relied on line of sight and were not secure.

BRUCE BAIRNSFATHER

The creator of the iconic cartoon 'Tommy' and 'Old Bill', the artist Bruce Bairnsfather served at Ypres and as a young officer in the Royal Warwickshire Regiment. He was nearly courtmartialled for taking part in the 'Christmas Truce' of 1914. While on the Western Front, Bairnsfather drew pictures of trench life.

Suffering from the effects of a chlorine gas attack in the wake of the Second Battle of Ypres in April 1915, Bairnsfather was subsequently wounded by a shell explosion and sent home to Britain to recuperate.

While at the London General Hospital he was diagnosed as suffering from the effects of shell shock. During his stay in hospital the *Bystander* magazine commissioned him to produce a series of weekly drawings that were subsequently published as the six-volume *Fragments from France* (selling over 250,000 copies). He also published two books on his war experiences, *Bullets & Billets* and *From Mud to Mufti*.

Bairnsfather's work was extremely popular with the soldiers in the trenches and this helped sales of the magazine. However, some people objected to his drawings and one member of the House of Commons condemned 'these vulgar caricatures of our heroes'.

With his recuperation complete the government dispatched Bairnsfather to the Isle of Wight to oversee the training of fresh recruits bound for France and Flanders. It was during this period that he created the character 'Old Bill', which rapidly brought its creator widespread praise and popularity.

The enduring cartoon of this period shows 'Bill' sheltering in a shell crater with another soldier and as shot and shell scream overhead 'Bill' utters the immortal words 'Well if you knows of a better 'ole go to it'.

20. An observation balloon used for spotting the fall of shot for the Royal Artillery. The British, however, did not deploy Kite balloons, as they were called, to France until May 1915.

Normally with flares a pre-arranged set of signals would have been laid down. Communication by field telephones was fast, but not reliable. Shell fire often cut the telephone lines, however deeply they were buried, and tracing and locating the break would mean that signallers had to cross exposed and dangerous terrain.

Dogs and pigeons were also used to carry messages. The French and Germans favoured dogs which presented less of a target and could carry bigger messages than a pigeon. The British favoured pigeons and it is reported that 95 per cent of their messages reached their destinations.

21. A painting of Private Gudgeon of 1st Battalion Northamptons who was awarded the DCM for his work as a runner and guide in the First Battle of Ypres. The job of a runner carrying messages and orders was lonely and dangerous, but vital.

The Days Before Battle

Once trench warfare had set in, it was easier in some respects to build up a picture of the battlefield. Both sides printed detailed trench maps showing the frontline and secondary trenches, communications trenches and other positions. Aerial photography ensured that these maps were up to date and accurate. Behind these field fortifications were dumps of stores and ammunition and some of the Commonwealth War Graves cemeteries bear their names because regimental aid posts and clearing stations were co-located.

What the days before battle were like depended on whether the soldier was going to be part of an offensive or whether he would be on the receiving end. For men destined to be attacked there might be unusual air activity as hostile commanders attempted to build up as detailed a picture as possible. The pattern of artillery

22. A postcard produced during the war showing 'A British sentry in Flanders'. The images permitted for the general public were sanitised and it was only after the war that many became aware of the full horror of life in the trenches.

fire might change as new batteries brought up to support the offensive registered their guns. Trench raids might be launched to gain localised intelligence and dominate no man's land and drive in the opposing patrols.

For men about to be part of an attack there would be briefings about objectives and also morale boosting pep talks. These could backfire when, having been promised a 'walk over', attacking troops found their way blocked by uncut wire and unsuppressed machine guns. From spring 1915 at Ypres some of the British attacks were preceded by the explosion of mines buried deep under German trench lines. For the troops waiting the detonation – far bigger than any weight of artillery – the sight was spectacular and reassuring. The artillery bombardment would follow and then the men would scramble up ladders that had been brought forward into the trenches and start the steady advance across no man's land towards the enemy.

THE BATTLEFIELDS:
WHAT ACTUALLY HAPPENED?

First Ypres

21–24 October	British 7th Division hold off repeated German assaults to east of Ypres	
24 October	Previous assaults having failed, Germans prepare for a concerted offensive on Ypres further south	

Germans prepare to launch attack between Gheluvelt and Messines

5.30am	German artillery bombardment commences
8am	German 54th Reserve Division and 30th Division attack the Gheluvelt–Zandvoorde line, with little effect on British defences, but inflicting serious casualties
10am	Germans advance to Zandvoorde village and enfilade infantry battalions
Afternoon	British establish a new line behind Zandvoorde and stabilise the front between there and Zillebeke; 7th Division withdraw and rest
Evening	British commanders assess situation; villages of Hollebeke and Zandvoorde have been lost; British line remains intact

29 October

Ypres 1914-15

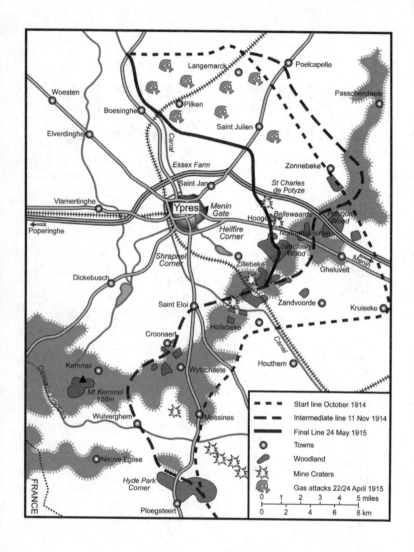

Legend:

- - - - Start line October 1914
- – – – Intermediate line 11 Nov 1914
- ──── Final Line 24 May 1915
- Towns
- Woodland
- Mine Craters
- Gas attacks 22/24 April 1915

```
0    1    2    3    4    5 miles
0      2      4      6      8 km
```

Map labels:

Woesten, Langemarck, Poelcapelle, Passchendaele, Boesinghe, Pilken, Elverdinghe, Saint Julien, Zonnebeke, Essex Farm, St Charles de Potyze, Vlamertinghe, Saint Jan, Canal, Ypres, Menin Gate, Hooge, Bellewaarde, Polygon Wood, Poperinghe, Hellfire Corner, Nonnebosschen, Sanctuary Wood, Shrapnel Corner, Zillebeke, Menin, Dickebusch, Gheluvelt, Saint Eloi, Zandvoorde, Kruiseke, Hollebeke, Croonaert, Houthem, Kemmel, Wytschaete, Mt Kemmel 156m, Canal, Casualle Corner, Wulverghem, Messines, Neuve Eglise, FRANCE, Hyde Park Corner, Ploegsteert

23. The experience and professionalism of the BEF were demonstrated by Corporal Redpath of 1st Battalion Royal Highlanders (The Black Watch) who won the DCM during the First Battle of Ypres in November 1914. He left his trench and closed with the enemy to ensure accurate shooting and convince the Germans that there was a stronger force in the area.

The First Battle of Ypres represented the last attempt by Allied and German forces to outflank each other and force a decisive breakthrough on the Western Front in 1914. Simultaneous advances met 'head on' and a series of bitterly contested actions followed in which superior German numbers forced the Allies into the fiercest of defensive battles. The fighting (in which French support was vital to British resistance) was widespread, desperate and continuous but three critical phases of action defined its progress.

In early October 1914 the BEF had relocated from the cramped stalemate on the River Aisne to Flanders, on the extreme left of the Allied line, and was encouraged to make offensive movements within the La Bassée sector and north to Ypres. These aggressive probings coincided with simultaneous German moves westward and a series of confusing encounter battles ensued in which the larger forces deployed by the Germans forced British withdrawals to an extended and thinly held line. Following the failure of German attempts in the north to force the Allied line along the coast, strong German forces were concentrated against Ypres in a search for a breakthrough to the Channel ports.

Between 21–24 October, whilst the British 7th Division held off repeated German assaults to the east of Ypres, British I Corps to the north-east collided with strong advancing concentrations of German troops around Langemarck. A series of determined defensive actions, in which fast and accurate rifle fire wreaked havoc against repeated German mass infantry attacks, prevented a breakthrough. The German offensive faltered and on the evening of 24 October preparations were made for a separate great assault on Ypres further south. This new attack between Gheluvelt and Messines began on 29 October and culminated in the crucial action on the 31st, which broke the British line. The initiative of local commanders and a bold attack by the 2nd Battalion Worcesters restored the situation. A third major German assault on Ypres took place on 11 November, when the Prussian Guard Division advanced along the Menin Road. This potentially decisive attack was checked by British field artillery and a hastily improvised rearguard force.

On the morning of 30 October the Allied commanders were totally unaware of the massing of important German reinforcements opposite the point at which the defences above Ypres were both strategically vital and tactically weak. The night of the 29th/30th had been relatively quiet and sounds of movement from the German side, heard by men in the frontline trenches, had been misinterpreted as indicating a possible German withdrawal. While Sir John French had seen no cause to alter his orders for continued attack, Sir Douglas Haig showed a more cautious approach, ordering the three divisions of I Corps to entrench on the favourable ground they held, re-organise and continue reconnaissance activity. This was to prove invaluable when the five new German divisions of Fabeck's Group, the presence of which was completely unknown to Allied intelligence, and which had relieved the German 6th Bavarian Reserve Division and the two northernmost divisions of the German Cavalry Corps, facing the

24. Field Marshal Sir Douglas Haig who commanded I Corps at Ypres and would eventually command the BEF. He was a highly educated commander who saw the potential of weapons like the tank and led the British to victory on the Western Front.

line from Zandvoorde to Gheluvelt, fell upon the British front. Fabeck's artillery, including 260 heavy and super-heavy guns, had moved into position and ranged during the 29th.

The Germans were in no doubt that this battle was to be decisive. Orders, issued on 29 October, were later found on the body of a dead German officer of the XV Corps. They concluded with:

> The break-through will be of decisive importance. We must and will therefore conquer, settle forever with the centuries-long struggle, end the war, and strike a blow against our most detested enemy. We will finish with the British, Indians, Canadians, Moroccans, and other trash, feeble adversaries, who surrender in great numbers if they are attacked with vigour.
>
> *British Official History*

The German Operation Orders were for an attack on the whole salient but stressed that the main effort would be made by Fabeck's Group, which attacked the area between the Menin

Road and Zandvoorde (inclusive). The Germans planned for the first objectives to be Zandvoorde and Messines, with the intention of achieving a breakthrough to the Kemmel heights.

From the beginning the attack did not go as the Germans had hoped. At 8am an attack by the 54th Reserve Division and the 30th Division against the Gheluvelt–Zandvoorde line failed to have the effect expected. Although both divisional generals went to the frontline to encourage their men, no impression could be made against the determined British defence. British losses, however, were serious, particularly in the infantry battalions of the 7th Division, where the trenches were on a forward slope. By 10am the Germans were pushing forward to Zandvoorde village from where they enfiladed the infantry battalions, which had already repulsed a direct attack from its front, with rifle and gunfire, causing great numbers of casualties.

British brigade and divisional commanders worked to establish a new line behind Zandvoorde. By the afternoon the line had stabilised between Zandvoorde and Zillebeke allowing the troops of 7th Division to withdraw and rest. The Germans showed little stomach to exploit their previous success and the new line was held, although the infantry battalions of the division had suffered grievously. 1st Royal Welsh Fusiliers ended the day with only eighty-six survivors. Among the dead was Lieutenant Colonel H.O.S. Cadogan, killed while tending to his injured adjutant. They lie side by side in the Hooge Crater cemetery.

By the end of the day General Headquarters (GHQ) was still in ignorance of precisely which German forces had attacked the 7th Division. The villages of Hollebeke and Zandvoorde had been lost, but the line was held. In the absence of Operation Orders from GHQ the battle on the 31st would lie in the hands of the corps commanders, Allenby and Haig. By the evening of the 30th four infantry battalions: 1st Grenadier Guards, 1st Coldstream Guards, 1st Royal Welsh Fusiliers and 2nd Wiltshire Regiment had been practically annihilated.

Gheluvelt

The First Battle of Ypres intensifies

31 October		
	Noon	British units: Queens, Royal Scots, Fusiliers, Welsh and Kings Royal Rifles are overwhelmed; on right of the line South Wales Borderers pushed back by German assault
	1pm	2nd Battalion, the Worcestershire Regiment ordered to attack and re-take village of Gheluvelt
	Afternoon	2nd Worcesters move from Polygon Wood towards Gheluvelt Château, overcoming German resistance and linking up with the South Wales Borderers
		British forces re-take Gheluvelt
		South-west of Gheluvelt newly arrived 129th Duke of Connaught's Own Baluchis deployed to support British defence are overwhelmed
		Germans overrun key British positions, but the line is held long enough for British and Indian units to reinforce, preventing German breakthrough

The crisis of the First Battle of Ypres hinged around the village of Gheluvelt. Lying on a forward spur of the low ridge that covers the town of Ypres, Gheluvelt was the last point retained in British hands from which the German line could be dominated. By noon on 31 October 1914, the Queens, the Royal Scots Fusiliers, the Welsh and the Kings Royal Rifles had been overwhelmed, while on the right the South Wales Borderers had been rolled back. Gheluvelt had been lost and a serious gap had been made in the British line. So serious was the situation that unless the gap could be closed, a breakthrough could not be avoided. Indeed orders had already been prepared for artillery to move back in preparation for a general retreat. On the evening of 30 October, the 2nd Battalion, the Worcestershire Regiment commanded by

Major E.B. Hankey remained uncommitted resting in Polygon Wood, all other units having been sent to reinforce the line.

The 2nd Worcesters were almost the last available reserve of the British defence. Nearly every other unit had been drawn into the battle line or suffered very heavy casualties. The 2nd Battalion, the Worcestershire Regiment had been through ten days of fighting and had been reduced to 500 haggard, unshaven and unwashed men in muddy and tattered uniforms. But their weapons were clean and in good order, they had plenty of ammunition, and three months of war had given them confidence in their fighting power. The short period in reserve had allowed them sleep and eat.

At 1pm on 31 October, the 2nd Battalion received an order to attack and retake Gheluvelt. From Polygon Wood the château which dominated the village could not be seen, but the nearby church tower rising amidst the smoke was visible. All around were wounded and stragglers coming to the rear and batteries could be seen limbering up and moving back. The Worcesters alone were moving towards the Germans.

As the leading men reached the ridge, they came in view of the German guns whose high explosive shells were quickly directed on the charging soldiers. Over 100 of the battalion were killed or wounded but the rest pushed on and, increasing their speed as they came to the downward slope in sight of Gheluvelt, made the final charge through hedges and on to the château grounds.

Beyond a little wood the battalion deployed, 'C' and 'D' companies in frontline, with 'B' Company in second line behind – about 370 men in total. In front of them rose the bare slope of the Polderhoek Ridge, littered with dead and wounded, and along its crest shells were bursting in rapid succession. Major Hankey decided that the only way of crossing that deadly stretch of ground was by one long rush. The companies extended into line and advanced.

The ground underfoot was rank grass or rough stubble. The two leading companies broke into a steady double (twice normal marching speed) and swept forward across the open, the officers leading on in front, and behind them their men with fixed bayonets in one long irregular line. As they reached the crest, the rushing wave of bayonets was sighted by the German gunners who opened fire with high explosive rounds and shrapnel. The speed of the rush increased as on the downward slope the troops came in sight of Gheluvelt Château close in front. The platoons scrambled across the light railway, through some hedges and wire fences, and then in the grounds of the château they closed with the Germans.

The German infantry were ill-prepared to meet the charge, as they were crowded in disorder among the trees of the park, their attention divided between exploring the outhouses and surrounding the remnant of the British defenders in the château. Their disorder was increased by the sharp and accurate fire of shrapnel from British batteries behind Polygon Wood.

The Germans were young troops of newly formed units (the 244th and 245th Reserve regiments and the 16th Bavarian Reserve Regiment). They probably had lost their best leaders earlier in the day, for they made no great attempt to stand their ground and face the counterattack. They gave way at once before the onslaught of the British battalion and crowded back out of the grounds of the château into the hedgerows beyond. Shooting and stabbing, C Company, led by Captain E.L. Bowring, closely followed by 2nd Lieutenant F.C.F. Biscoe charged across the lawn and came up into line with the survivors of the South Wales Borderers.

The meeting of the two battalions was unexpected. The Worcesters had not known that any of the South Wales Borderers were still holding out. Hankey went over to their commander and found him to be Colonel H.E. Burleigh Leach, an old friend. With characteristic British understatement Hankey greeted Leach 'My God, fancy meeting you here', and the exhausted Leach replied quietly 'Thank God you have come'.

However, the village of Gheluvelt, on the slope above the right flank, was still held by the Germans. Most of the German troops in the village seemed to have been drawn northwards by the fighting around the château, but a certain number of 'Saxons' of the 242nd Regiment had remained in the village. To silence their fire Hankey sent fighting patrols, which drove back the German snipers and took some prisoners. To secure the area he ordered A Company to advance from their defensive position and occupy the village and, after some sharp fighting among burning buildings and bursting shells, the company occupied a new line with its left flank in touch with the right of the position in the sunken road and its right flank in the village, holding the church and churchyard. Finally, he sent forward patrols to clear the village.

The German forces made no further effort that day to retake Gheluvelt. The reason for their inaction is not clear. It is possible that the very boldness of the counterattack may have given them the impression that the battalion was but the first wave of a stronger force, and the Germans may have stood on the defensive to meet that imagined attack. Furthermore the British maintained heavy artillery fire throughout the afternoon on the low ground east of Gheluvelt, which may have disorganised the Germans and which probably hampered the transmission of information and orders. Indeed the vagueness of most German accounts of the fighting at Gheluvelt suggests that the position in the village was not ascertained. In such circumstances, with the situation obscure, young troops discouraged and hostile shell fire unsubdued, it is no easy matter to organise a fresh attack. Perhaps some commander of importance was disabled or some vital line of communication severed. Whatever the reason, the result was that the German action during the rest of the day was limited to a violent bombardment, which had little effect.

Elsewhere fighting was fierce to the south-west of Gheluvelt where the newly arrived 129th Duke of Connaught's Own Baluchis had been rushed to the frontline to support the hard-pressed British troops. On 31 October, two companies of the Baluchis bore the brunt of the main German attack. The outnumbered Baluchis fought gallantly but were overwhelmed after suffering heavy casualties.

Sepoy Khudadad Khan's machine gun team, along with one other, kept their guns in action throughout the day, preventing the

25. *The first man from the Indian sub-continent to be awarded the Victoria Cross, Sepoy Khudadad Khan kept his machine gun in action in fighting at Klein Zillebeke on 31 October 1914 and imposed a critical delay on the German advance.*

Germans from making the final breakthrough. The other gun was disabled by a shell and eventually Khudadad Khan's own crew was overrun. All the men were shot or bayoneted except Khudadad Khan, who despite being badly wounded had continued firing his machine gun. When the Germans finally overran the position the 26-year-old was left for dead, but despite his wounds he managed to crawl back to his regiment during the night. Thanks to his bravery, and that of his fellow Baluchis, the Germans were held up just long enough for Indian and British reinforcements to arrive. They strengthened the line and prevented the German Army from reaching the vital ports. For his matchless feat of courage and gallantry, Sepoy Khudadad Khan was awarded the Victoria Cross (VC) and became the first South Asian soldier to be awarded the honour (native Indian officers and other ranks had only become eligible for the award of the VC in 1912). Unlike many VC recipients in the First World War he survived to die of old age in Pakistan in 1971.

The Wider Battle

20 October

I Corps (Haig) deploys to Ypres

II Corps (Smith-Dorrien) face assault by five German corps of Fourth German Army

2nd Royal Irish, 8th Brigade, 3rd Division at Le Pilly forced to surrender to Germans

British 6th Division suffer heavy losses during retreat to La Valle

II Corps abandon La Bassée

Evening: I Corps arrive to bolster British defence

21 October

Germans attack 3rd Division, who are forced to retreat

12th Brigade succeed in securing Le Gheer, despite temporary loss to the Germans

Germans open temporary gap in 19th Brigade's left flank, which is secured by midnight

Germans threaten left flank of 1st Cavalry Division, but they hold their position at Messines Ridge

3rd Cavalry Brigade, 2nd Cavalry Division forced from Kortewilde by shelling, retreat to Hollebeke Château; confusion causes other units to retreat, but lost ground is regained quickly

21 October

5th Division's line is broken at Poezelhoek by Germans

2nd Brigade is forced to withdraw from Zonnebeke Château

I Corps advance to Thourout, but are repelled by German defence

French Cavalry Corps forced back to the Yser Canal

2nd Division, I Corps forced to halt its advance by German resistance

Sir John French issues order for British to dig-in positions

The wider battle had begun while Haig's I Corps was en route to Ypres, arriving to the west of the town during 20 October. Smith-Dorrien's corps, to the north, was left facing the full force of five German corps of the German Fourth Army. The initial German attack, owing to French's orders to advance, caught II Corps without any defensive preparation. Surrender was the only option for the men of the 2nd Royal Irish Regiment of the 8th Brigade, 3rd Division who were cut off and surrounded at the village of Le Pilly. They fought hard and one battalion of 578 was reduced to 257 men and the casualties included the commanding officer. The 290 wounded men who survived became prisoners. It was little consolation that the staff of the 3rd Division had recognised the Royal Irish were too far forward and had intended to pull them back. II Corps and particularly 5th Division were forced to abandon La Bassée. However that night they learned that I Corps had reached Ypres.

The 6th Division under General J.L. Keir was very severely mauled in the retreat to La Valle. German formations approached in the afternoon, and at dusk the German 26th Division of XIII Corps, supported by the German 25th Reserve Division, caught the British infantry in shallow trenches. In a two-night battle, the Sherwood Foresters were overwhelmed by superior German numbers. In the retreat to La Valle, some survivors had been intercepted by advanced German elements. In the confusion, German formations were mistaken for being British reinforcements. The battalion suffered heavy casualties, including many captured, and was destroyed.

A further German attack on 21 October, stronger than the one that had destroyed the Royal Irish, developed against 5th Division.

26. German prisoners carry a wounded British soldier – who according to the wartime caption told the photographer 'I'm not a German!' Wounds that would not be fatal today could be killers in a world with no antibiotics.

It was ordered to retreat to a more suitable, less exposed defensive line that evening. Thus began a 2½-mile retreat to a hastily prepared line on 22/23 October. The retirement of the 5th Division was covered by the 3rd Lahore Division under General Watkis, part of the Indian Corps. Smith-Dorrien was given orders that these were operational reserve units only and he was not to engage them unless there was no other recourse. Elsewhere on 21 October, 12th Brigade under Brigadier Aylmer Hunter-Weston succeeded in inflicting heavy casualties on German infantry attempting to take Le Gheer, some 5 miles due south of Ypres, near the French border. It was briefly lost, but secured by dark, when 1st Battalion, Somerset Light Infantry and 1st Battalion, East Lancashire Regiment recaptured the ground lost. Some 160 German prisoners were taken. The German tactic of massing men in columns meant that they suffered severely. Towards the end of First Ypres, German tactical formations changed and infantry began to advance in small 'blobs' or 'swarms'. The Germans succeeded in opening a gap on the 19th Brigade's left flank at Le Maisnil, which was partially closed by midnight.

The left flank of General de Lisle's 1st Cavalry Division had been threatened by the German attack and penetration, but it held its position on the Messines Ridge despite thinning its ranks. Shell fire drove Gough's 3rd Cavalry Brigade of his 2nd Cavalry Division out of its positions at Kortewilde. The line was pulled back to Hollebeke Château. However some units thought that Gough's order was for a general retreat beyond Hollebeke Château to new positions. Once this was realised, Gough ordered an immediate counterattack to recapture any lost ground, which succeeded against the German Cavalry Corps with low casualties. The 6th Cavalry Brigade and Capper's 7th British Division then moved to cover the gap that threatened Gough's left flank.

Covering some 5½ miles of front the 7th Division were now overstretched and bent at right angles around Kruiseecke. The men had few entrenching tools with which to dig in and increase the strength of the position. Unfortunately it was only partially concealed at the foot of the German-held ridges at Becelaere and Passchendaele, and the divisional commander and his subordinates, through lack of experience, did not recognise that they were in a poor location. The Germans managed to break through at Poezelhoek at the junction between 20th and 21st brigades. Heavy attacks at Poldserhoek were held by the tough soldiers of the 2nd Battalion, Royal Scots Fusiliers. It was in the afternoon that the presence of I Corps began to be felt as it advanced on the north flank of IV Corps and Capper was able to spare units to cover the gap caused by the withdrawal of the 3rd Cavalry Brigade. During the course of the days fighting, there was only one minor retreat; the 22nd Brigade's withdrawal from Zonnebeke Château.

French believed that only one German Corps opposed I Corps and Haig pushed towards Thourout in an effort to follow French's orders for offensive action, but found German resistance too strong to make any gains. Similarly the French Cavalry Corps, on the left of Haig's 1st Division, was forced back to the Yser Canal in the face of strong opposition from the German 46th Reserve Division of General von Kleist's XXII Reserve Corps. The 2nd Division did not fair much better, advancing some 1,000–2,000 yards before being stopped by German artillery.

Bad weather prevented reconnaissance flights by the Royal Flying Corps (RFC); nevertheless, the amount of opposition and German prisoners indicated the German forces were concentrating against the BEF. In fact the German Fourth Army's

ROYAL FLYING CORPS

When war broke out Britain had about 113 aircraft in service with the Royal Flying Corps (RFC). In contrast the German Air Service had 246 and the French Aviation Service 160. In four years aircraft changed from fragile single or two-seater single engined machines to four engined multi-crew bombers capable of lifting a 1,000lb bomb.

When the RFC deployed to France in 1914 it sent four squadrons, numbers 2, 3, 4 and 5, each with twelve aircraft – which when aircraft in depots were included made up a force of sixty-three machines supported by 900 men. There was a wide variety of aircraft types. By September 1915 and the Battle of Loos, RFC strength stood at twelve squadrons and 161 aircraft. A little under a year later at the first Battle of the Somme the RFC had more than doubled, with twenty-seven squadrons, 421 aircraft and a further 216 in depots. Aircraft construction and pilot selection and training came under considerable pressure as the RFC expanded so rapidly.

XVII Reserve Corps (von Carlowitz) was opposite IV Corps, and elements of its XXIII and XXVI Reserve Corps opposite I Corps. The French and Belgians were assailed by elements of XXIII Corps, III and XXII Reserve Corps. To the south of Ypres, the German Sixth Army deployed VII Corps against Smith-Dorrien's II Corps and its XIII Corps and XIX (Saxon) Corps were engaging III British Corps and Conneau's French Cavalry Corps. The German I, IV and V Cavalry corps were opposite Allenby's Cavalry Corps. At this point, seven and one-third British divisions, reduced by fighting, and five Allied cavalry divisions being used as infantry, were holding a front of 36 miles against eleven German divisions, eight of which were fresh, supported by eight cavalry divisions.

Sir John French finally accepted that offensive operations were impossible under present conditions and issued a general order to dig in. It appears that the Germans did not know that the BEF was understrength and overstretched and vulnerable to a concentrated attack, on most parts of the line. The ferocity of the British defence had convinced the Germans that there were strong Allied entrenched positions at Ypres. In fact there were only small groups of infantry spread thin, with trenches no more than 3ft deep, without wire or dugouts. So sparse was machine gun and artillery fire, the only way to cover gaps in the line was with crossfire.

The Langemarck Legend

22 October

D'Urbal orders the French troops to counterattack German XXIII Corps, near Dixmude

French Cavalry Corps, 42nd French Division and Belgian Army Detachment passed through British 1st Division lines on their march to Dixmude

French force are repulsed by Germans and retreat back through British positions between Langemarck and Steenstraat

German XXIII Corps shell Langemarck heavily

British 5th Brigade, 2nd Division, force back advancing Germans and hold the town

October 22 marked the birth of the legend of Langemarck. On November 11, 1914, the German OHL (High Command) issued a communiqué stating that young German soldiers, many of them student volunteers, had marched into action singing the national anthem '*Deutschland, Deutschland über alles, über alles in der Welt*' but in the subsequent fighting had suffered heavy losses. The fighting had taken place near Bikschote but the OHL favoured the name of the village of Langemarck as the site of the battle – it sounded more Germanic. According to regimental histories the song was actually '*Wacht am Rhein*' - Watch on the Rhine, and it was sung only for identification as units moved through heavy mist. Several German regiments (206th Reserve Infantry Regiment and 204th Reserve Infantry Regiment) are on record as singing this in battle when attacking 1st Division. Indeed throughout the 1914 battles, German regimental histories made constant reference to recognition songs. German casualties were heavy in assaults on the 1st Division. Some German units, over several days fighting, may have lost 70 per

D'URBAL

A dashing cavalryman, d'Urbal's star seemed to be in the ascendancy with promotion from brigadier to general at the beginning of the First World War. He had been in command of the 7th Cavalry Division on 25 August but by 20 September was commanding the XXXIII Army Corps. A month later, on 20 October he was given command of the French troops in Belgium and then on 16 November the Eighth Army. Command of the Tenth Army which he was given on 2 April 1915 was his undoing. Following the battle of La Bassée in May–July and the Artois in September–October 1915, he was dismissed on 4 April 1916 and four days later appointed Inspector General of Cavalry of the war zone. His appointment as Inspector General of Cavalry Reserves and of the Interior on 28 February 1917 was in effect a further demotion.

cent of their effective strength to British rifle fire. In the Second World War in 1940 the German cemetery at Langemarck would be visited by Hitler who served as a junior NCO on the Ypres Salient. Later, the 27th Waffen-SS Volunteer Division that recruited from Flemish speakers in Belgium and Holland would be named Langemarck.

French had decided to stay on the defensive; however, in the south the French forces, commanded by the newly promoted 'Commander of the North' General Victor d'Urbal, were ordered to counterattack against the German XXIII Corps that was advancing on Dixmude, a town east of Nieuport and south of Ostend. De Mitry's Cavalry Corps, the 42nd French Division and the French Detachment in Belgium, renamed the French Eighth Army in November, would have to pass through British 1st Division lines to launch this attack – it failed and French forces were driven back through British lines between Langemarck and Steenstraat.

Gunners from the advancing German XXIII Corps shelled Langemarck heavily when it came into contact with the unsupported British 1st Division. The 5th Brigade of the 2nd British Division moved to plug the gaps caused by the retreating French and, through aimed and rapid rifle fire, succeeded in repulsing German infantry attempting to overrun the town. The Germans made a last assault that night, setting farms alight to give their gunners reference points. The attack launched at close range proved to be a disaster for the Germans. At first light ad hoc British battlegroups launched counterattacks that recaptured lost ground, captured 800 Germans and even released British soldiers taken prisoner in earlier fighting. Incredibly for British losses of 47 dead and 187 wounded, some 500 Germans had been killed. To the right of 2nd Division there was an early example of the value of air reconnaissance when RFC aircraft spotted the approach of German columns advancing in open formation towards Becelaere and they were shot down in large numbers by the 21st Brigade.

The arrival of French reinforcements and German losses convinced the German operations staff that a breakthrough was not likely in the immediate future. Grossetti's French 42nd Division, which joined the Belgian Army at Nieuport, and the 17th and 18th French divisions of the French IX Corps under General Dubois, which was arriving west and south of Ypres, were to relieve the I Corps which was under heavy pressure. Following these reinforcements, d'Urbal and Foch, commanding the French armies in the north, agreed with Sir John French to launch a general offensive. The Belgians and 42nd

MARTIN-LEAKE

It was in fighting near Zonnebeke between 29 October and 8 November that Lieutenant Arthur Martin-Leake RAMC attached to 5th Field Ambulance would achieve an almost unique distinction. Martin-Leake would be one of only three men to win a Bar to his VC and the only man do so in two wars. On 8 February 1902 as a 27-year-old Surgeon Captain with the South African Constabulary he had been awarded the VC at Vlakfontein in the Transvaal. Here he had risked his life to tend to wounded soldiers in open ground under fire from forty Boer riflemen – he had only ceased this work when he had been hit three times and was completely exhausted and refused water until all the other wounded had been served.

After the Boer War, Martin-Leake went to work as a doctor on the Indian railways. In 1914 – now aged forty – he travelled to Paris and enlisted at the British Consulate and then attached himself to the first medical unit he could find. Between 29 October and 8 November he was back in the thick of fighting and personally rescued many wounded men lying close to German positions and under heavy fire. This period of sustained selfless courage and care for others earned him the bar to his VC.

Incredibly he survived the war retiring with the rank of Lieutenant Colonel and returned to work on the Indian railways until his retirement in 1932. He died in 1953 and is buried at St John's Church, High Cross, Hertfordshire – his almost unique decoration is displayed at the Royal Army Medical Corps museum.

Division would advance eastward from Nieuport with the support of British naval gunfire. The Dixmude garrison would take Thourout, and Guignabaudet's 17th Division, with two of de Mitry's cavalry divisions would push towards the rail hub at Roulers in order to reach the Passchendaele–Becelaere line. Owing to German offensive operations, the offensive was delayed.

Nonnebosschen

11 November		12½ German divisions launch attack on 9-mile British front between Messines and Reutel
	9am	Heavy German artillery barrage commences
		Germans advance rapidly, but make little headway
		German 4th Division breaches the line at Menin Road, held by British II Corps
	c.10am	Germans push through to Nonnebosschen, held by 1st and 3rd Foot Guards Regiment, artillery fire from both British and German batteries halts their advance.
		British reserves are ordered to form up and are deployed to Polygon Wood
		1st Battalion, Buckinghamshires and Ox and Bucks troops, supported by artillery, repulse the Germans from the woods surrounding Nonnebosschen
		The British line is secured

The Germans outnumbered the Allies, but their infantry were using the tactics of earlier centuries and marching into the attack in close order, which caused unnecessary casualties. At higher levels, commanders like Fabeck and Albrecht, GOC Fourth Army, continued with the attack despite rising casualties and attempted to apply pressure to the north of Ypres, on the Comines Canal. In these attacks they were supported by Group Gerok, an ad hoc formation, comprising the 3rd Division, 25th Reserve Division, 11th Landwehr Brigade and the 6th Bavarian Reserve Division.

27. Cavalry troops patrol along the flooded Yperlee Canal, Ypres. The Great War was to prove that the role of the cavalry, if not obsolete, was certainly rendered to the sidelines in a static warfare of trenches and machine guns. (New York Times, 03/21/1915 Courtesy of the Great War Photo Archive: www.gwpda.org.uk)

Though fighting had been limited during early November, the 3rd and 26th German divisions did break through to St Eloi and advance to Zwarteleen, some 3,000 yards east of Ypres, but were checked by the British 7th Cavalry Brigade. On 10 November the Germans attacked French and Belgian forces between Langemarck and Dixmude, forcing them back to the Yser Canal. However, the Belgians blew all the weirs and bridges on the river.

On 11 November there was an assault by twelve and a half German divisions from Group Fabeck, the German Fourth and Sixth Armies, and XXVII Reserve Corps. The heavy bombardment kept the Allied infantry pinned down as German infantry advanced, but they were slow and return fire was possible.

The main weight of the German attack came opposite the Gheluvelt, extending from the so-called Shrewsbury Forest in the south, across the Menin Road, to Nonnebosschen (Nun's Copse) and the edge of Polygon Wood beyond it. This feature was held by the exhausted 2nd Division, who were defending a 3,500-yard front. The total strength of the division was 7,000 men, of whom 2,000 were reserves, and they were up against twenty-five German battalions of 17,500. Under sheer weight of numbers the British fell back on hastily improvised strong points. The German 4th Division broke into the forward trenches which the British failed to recover during counterattacks. However, strong points held and prevented any serious breach and rifle fire repulsed German attacks between Polygon Wood and Veldhoek.

When the Germans reached Nonnebosschen they were faced by the British 4th Guards Brigade; a force of no more than 900 men. British artillery that had been held in reserve due to ammunition shortages opened fire and this prevented the Germans from launching a concentrated attack. At this stage the artillery lines were the last line of defence for Ypres. Monro, GOC II Corps, ordered his reserves, the Irish Guards and the 2nd Battalion, Oxfordshire and Buckinghamshire Light Infantry (Ox and Bucks), to form up and be ready to move. The 2nd Battalion, Highland Light Infantry was ordered was to reinforce the distinctive feature of Polygon Wood. It was now partially occupied by German formations and the Ox and Bucks' commanding officer Lieutenant Colonel Henry Davies was ordered to clear it. This was some 7 miles away to the east and Davies decided the breach at Nonnebosschen was more pressing. With the Ox and Bucks and artillery support from the 39th Brigade Royal Field Artillery, he attacked and pushed the Germans out of the surrounding forests near Nonnebosschen, catching many, including the six foot tall soldiers of the Prussian Guard, by surprise. The British reached the forward trenches but were then shelled by the French in error. In November 1965 the Sergeants Mess of the 1st Battalion, The Royal Green Jackets, descendants of the Ox and Bucks and then part of the West Berlin garrison, invited veterans of the Prussian Guard to drinks. A small but superbly turned out group of six foot septuagenarians arrived, enjoyed the hospitality of the mess and at dawn departed – still looking immaculate.

28. *As the only survivor of his machine gun section Quartermaster Sergeant Downs of 1st Battalion, Cheshires manned a gun and beat off German attacks in November 1914 until reinforcements arrived. He was awarded the DCM.*

Ypres was secured from further attack and the Ypres-Comines canal front was not breached. The cost to the Ox and Bucks had been five dead and twenty-five wounded. Other units in the area suffered heavily, as had the attacking Germans. The German 4th Division suffered 2,932 casualties in November.

After heavy fighting and the virtual destruction of the BEF, Haig feared that the front was on the verge of collapse. In the event he was not to know that the battle was effectively over. On 17 November German commander Albrecht ordered his army to cease offensive operations and dig in where it stood. This order was immediately confirmed by Falkenhayn. III Reserve Corps under von Beseler and XIII Corps under Fabeck were ordered to

29. *Lieutenant John Dimmer of the 2nd Battalion, Kings Royal Rifle Corps cleared jams in a machine gun on three occasions but suffered multiple wounds including a round that stuck him in the jaw during fighting on 12 November, 1914 at Klein Zillebeke. He was awarded the Victoria Cross.*

the Eastern Front. The casualties, and the political and military situation on the Eastern Front was serious, particularly with the Russian concentration around Warsaw. Falkenhayn noted that the German Army in the West was exhausted and a quick decisive victory was no longer attainable.

The cost to the BEF for the stalemate of First Ypres was heavy, between 14 October and 30 November 1914: 2,298 officers and 51,807 men were killed, wounded or went missing.

Relative Quiet

The British Army used the 'relative quietness' of the winter 1914–15 to regroup. On 25 December an informal truce was observed and in places along the front, German and British soldiers met in no man's land swapping rations and drink, and in some places playing football. Many Germans had worked in Britain before the war in service industries and consequently had a passable command of English. In one conversation on Christmas Day a German asked if a British soldier would pass on a letter to his girlfriend in Manchester, while a Londoner discovered that his father's cobblers shop on the Essex Road was opposite the barber's shop where a German soldier had worked. The truce allowed both sides to collect their dead and give them a

30. A cross, footballs and a Christmas tree mark one of the places where the Christmas Truce of 1914 broke out spontaneously. This location is south of Ypres – whether a football match was played here between the Germans and British is open to speculation.

proper burial in the temporary cemeteries that were being dug. Corporal Arthur Cook of 1st Battalion, Somerset Light Infantry recalled that the Germans in the trenches opposite his battalion handed over the body of a young Somersets' captain and 'told us he was a very brave man'. Major R.T. Fellowes of 1st Battalion, Rifle Brigade had the curious experience of finding some sections behaving as if Christmas was another ordinary day in the trenches with routine work being undertaken, while in another the German and British soldiers were not only talking in no man's land, but working together to dig three mass graves, collect the bodies and give them a proper burial.

On Boxing Day in some sectors it was back to business as usual while in others, though there was no open fraternisation, the truce continued for several more days. There were few Christmas truces in the years that followed, though a 'live and let live' attitude generally prevailed on 25 December. Corporal Charlie Parke of 2nd Battalion, Gordon Highlanders remembered that 'Christmas

CLAY KICKERS

The driving force behind the establishment of a specialist force of mining troops known as 'Clay Kickers' or 'Moles' was Major John Norton Griffiths MP. He recruited men who had previously worked in the coal and tin mines and they began the hazardous process of digging shafts under German lines. While the underlying geology of some parts of the Western Front was chalk, in other parts there was soil and clay. Different techniques were developed for digging – however the most important feature was that they had to make a minimum of noise since this could be picked up by German listening devices. Entrenching tools, bayonets and specialist spades were used for digging and the 'Clay Kickers' had a cross-shaped bench that they braced themselves against as they dug out the shafts. Though the job was very well paid it was also very risky with both sides attempting to destroy or collapse shafts by counter-mining and detonating explosive charges known as 'camouflets'.

31. A modern sculpture of an Australian miner in Vierstraat, Wytschaete. Men used a variety of tools to dig the shafts – the figure has an entrenching tool – and looks very clean and tidy for a job that was dirty, hot and at times terrifying.

was the time by which many had expected to be home but now, as I peered across the 300 yards of no-man's-land that morning, I knew it was going to be a long, long haul'.

'Relative quietness' is as the words imply – relative – and in the spring fierce fighting took place for a 60m high feature to the south-east of Ypres, known to the British as Hill 60. In reality it was a low ridge some 150ft high and about 250 yards from end to end. It was artificially formed when the railway cutting was dug, which divided it into two distinct locations. The Germans had captured the ridge from the French on 10 December 1914 and soon after the British took over in February 1915 it was decided that this tactically significant ground had to be recaptured. The day selected for the attack – 17 April 1915 was quiet and hot, with brilliant sunshine. At 7pm, two pairs and a single mine dug by 171 Tunnelling Company were exploded under the hill at 10-second intervals. For an officer standing close to Corporal T. Newell from 171 Company it was a grim payback. 'We all just stood looking' recalled Newell 'And the officer beside me, the one who'd pushed the plunger, I heard him say, "There! That's avenged my brother"'.

32. Hill 60. This bunker constructed by the Australians is built on top of an existing German structure that had disappeared into the ground following mine blasts and shell fire. The exterior shows the distinctive ripple effect of corrugated galvanised iron shuttering. German bunkers have a smoother finish being constructed with wooden shuttering.

Lieutenant J. Todd of 11th Battalion, Prince of Wales' Own Yorkshire Regiment recalled the seconds before the mines exploded:

> It was an appalling moment. We all had the feeling, 'It's not going!' And then a most remarkable thing happened. The ground on which I was lying started to go up and down just like an earthquake. It lasted for seconds and then, suddenly in front of us, the Hill 60 mine went up.
>
> from Lyn Macdonald, *They Called It Passchendaele*

Immediately, the 1st Battalion, Royal West Kent Regiment and Royal Engineer (RE) Sappers charged forward. Within 3 minutes they had captured the crest and the engineers immediately started building field fortifications around the lips of the craters.

At around 8pm German artillery opened fire, with at one stage the fire coming from fifty-four different guns. This was

33. The savage fight in the south-east corner of Hill 60 on the night of 20 April 1915 in which 2nd Lieutenant Geoffrey Woolley became the first Territorial Force officer to win the Victoria Cross. Woolley would serve as an army chaplain in the Second World War.

followed by a counterattack. Hand-to-hand fighting took place with bayonet and bomb. Early in the morning a battalion of the King's Own Scottish Borderers moved up to the shell-pocked and cratered feature at the same time that the Germans put in another counterattack.

By the time they were withdrawn the West Kents had suffered 50 per cent casualties. In the days that followed battalions were rotated through the feature. On 20–21 April the fighting was particularly savage and it was then that four Victoria Crosses were won: Private E. Dwyer, Lieutenant Roupell, 2nd Lieutenant Geary and Lieutenant Woolley. Woolley from 1/9th Battalion, London

Regiment (Queen Victoria Rifles) was a Territorial soldier who had planned to join the church before the war. He survived the war and was ordained, serving as an army chaplain in North Africa in the Second World War.

On 1 May 1915 the Germans launched another attack backed by gas. The British battalion holding the hill on that day was the 1st Battalion, Dorsets with 59 Field Company (RE). When the gas cleared five officers and 300 men had become casualties. Another gas attack that followed four days later caught the 2nd Battalion, Duke of Wellingtons in the trenches. The battalion was overwhelmed and the top of the hill, such as it was, was captured by the Germans and remained in their hands with the British holding the trenches lower down.

After the war the Queen Victoria Rifles erected a monument at Hill 60. In 1940 when the area was captured by the Germans in the Second World War they destroyed it.

Second Ypres

The year 1915 saw the introduction of two new forms of warfare. Firstly there was gas, which signalled the commencement of the Second Battle of Ypres. Secondly flamethrowers ('liquid fire') at Hooge (30/31 July), although strictly this action is not part of Second Ypres it does give some idea of what is meant by 'relative quietness' in the Ypres sector.

At this time on the northern flank of the salient were the Belgians; covering the northern part of the salient itself were two French divisions: the 87th Metropolitan and the 45th Algerian. The eastern part of the salient was defended by the newly arrived Canadian Division and two British divisions. In all, the British forces in the Ypres area were the II and V corps of the Second Army made up of the 1st, 2nd and 3rd Cavalry divisions, and the 4th, 27th, 28th, 50th, Lahore and 1st Canadian divisions.

FIRE

The Germans were the first to use flamethrowers –
Flammenwerfer – with greatest effect during fighting
at Hooge on 30 July 1915. To Lieutenant Gordon Carey
of 8th Battalion, Rifle Brigade the first encounter
with the weapon was terrifying.

When the thing happened, so dramatically and so suddenly that
at first I was quite incapable of any comprehensive thought at
all. The first idea that flitted through my mind was that the end
of the world had come, and this was the Day of Judgement,
because the whole dawn had turned a ghastly crimson red.

from *Forgotten Voices of the Great War*

The German Army had tested two models of
Flammenwerfer in the early 1900s, one large and one
small. In the *Kleinflammenwerfer* – small flamethrower
or '*Kleif*' – fuel was stored in a large vertical, cylindrical
backpack container. High-pressure propellant was
stored in another, smaller container attached to the
fuel tank. A long hose connected the fuel tank to a
lance tube with an igniting device at the nozzle. The
propellant forced the fuel through the hose and out
of the nozzle at high speed when a valve was opened.
The igniting device at the nozzle set fire to the fuel as
it sprayed out. The flamethrower was operated by two
soldiers, one carrying the fuel and propellant tank. It
had a range of 82ft (25 metres).

The large flamethrower – *Grossflammenwerfer* or
'*Groß*' – was designed to be a static system to be used
from the trenches. The fuel and propellant containers
were too large and heavy for mobility, but the hose
could be long enough to be carried out of the trenches
closer to the enemy. Multiple propellant and fuel
containers could be connected together to improve
range and usage time. It had a range of 131ft (40
metres) and a burst that lasted for 40 seconds.

While unquestionably a formidable and terrifying
weapon, the man-portable flamethrower had a short
range, which meant that the operator had to get close
to his target – making him vulnerable to small arms fire.

Gravenstafel

First chlorine gas attack launched by Germans

22 April		
	5pm	Germans launch artillery bombardment
		British troops identify gas cloud emanating from German frontline
		Casualties inflicted on French and Colonial troops
		Canadians attempt to hold the line as troops retreat in the face of the gas attack
		Germans attack Langemarck village, but are counterattacked by 14th Battalion, 3rd Canadian Brigade
	6.30pm	Germans attempting to exploit gaps in the line created by the gas attack are stopped by Canadian artillery fire
		Canadian troops reinforce the defence positions around Ypres
	11pm	10th and 16th battalions, 2nd Canadian Brigade launch counterattack into gaps at Kitchener's Wood; they succeed in covering the gap, but sustain heavy losses

At around 5pm on 22 April 1915, the character of war changed forever when the German Army released 168 tons of chlorine gas along a 4-mile (6.5km) front held by French Territorial and Algerian troops of the 45th and 87th divisions. The attack came as a terrifying surprise to the French and British – and yet it should not have.

Incredibly *The Times* in London had published a short article on Friday 9 April 1915:

> It has been reported that in the Argonne, where the trenches are very close, the Germans have on several occasions pumped blazing oil or pitch onto the French, but, according to the

113

statements of our prisoners, they are preparing a more novel reception for us in front of parts of our line. They propose to asphyxiate our men if they advance by means of poisonous gas. The gas is contained under pressure in steel cylinders, and, being of a heavy nature, will spread along the ground without being dissipated quickly.

The Times, 9 April 1915

On 13 April a German soldier Private August Jaeger climbed out of his frontline trench and scrambled across the few hundred metres of no man's land, making for the French frontline. Jaeger had been called up on 4 August 1914. On 9 November he was attached as an automobile driver to the 234th Reserve Infantry Regiment (51st Reserve Division). For whatever reason, he decided to desert his post. He was interrogated by an officer of the French 11th Division and told him:

An attack is planned for the near future against the French trenches of the above mentioned sector. With this object in view four batteries have been placed in position in the first line trenches [in other words the trenches held by the men in Jaeger's company]; these batteries each have 20 bottles of asphyxiating gas. Each Company has 4 such batteries. Each battery has 5 gunners. At a given signal – 3 red rockets fired by the artillery – the bottles are uncorked, and the gas on escaping, is carried by a favourable wind towards the French trenches. This gas is intended to asphyxiate the men who occupy the trenches and to allow the Germans to occupy them without losses. In order to prevent the men being themselves intoxicated by the gas, each man is provided with a packet of tow steeped in oxygen. Since yesterday (13th inst.), all trains and convoys in position at ROULERS and RUMBEKE have been warned to be ready.

   Companies are about 160 strong on an average and are mostly commanded by active Army Lieutenants.

Official History of the Canadian Forces in the Great War, Vol 1

34. Looking like strange rodents in their P Helmets or Tube Helmet gas masks, a ration party of the King's Royal Rifle Corps is directed by 2nd Lieutenant Edward Allfrey to move through a gas saturated area. The P Helmet was introduced in July 1915.

The 11th Divisional commander, General Ferry, passed a warning to flanking units and to his own superior, General Balfourier, commander of the French XX Corps. Balfourier was highly sceptical, believing Ferry had been taken in. A staff officer from Grand Quartier Général was not only dismissive but scathing, since Ferry had passed his warning to the British on his right flank, ignoring the correct chain of communication between the British and the French. In any case, GHQ seems to have paid no attention to the warnings. Significantly Ferry was to hand over to the Canadian 1st Division on 17 April, as part of the move to extend the British V Corps' area of responsibility.

Research later showed that Jaeger's information was not the only warning. The French Tenth Army, on the right of the BEF, had issued a bulletin on 30 March, claiming that German XV Corps' prisoners had revealed that large stocks of cylinders containing asphyxiating gas had been placed near Zillebeke with the intention of mounting a gas attack.

On 16 April information was passed from the Belgian Army to the French that the Germans had manufactured 20,000 'mouth protectors... to protect the men against the effects of asphyxiating gas'. These reports were not entirely disregarded, although the French believed them to be a ruse designed to keep Allied troops from the Ypres area being deployed to aid the coming attacks in the Arras area. The reports were translated and circulated within GHQ on the 15th and 17th, but the idea was chiefly regarded as a French problem. Plumer at V Corps, next to the French, passed a warning to his divisional commanders 'for what it was worth', however, as nothing unusual occurred it was both disregarded and forgotten as attention was taken by the novelty of a German 17in. howitzer which now began to shell the town of Ypres, the shells travelling through the air with a sound 'like a runaway tramcar on badly laid rails'.

To prepare for the attack the Germans had moved 5,730 90lb metal cylinders, containing 168 tonnes of chlorine gas, through the narrow communications trenches and up to the frontline. On receipt of the signal soldiers also opened the valves on the cylinders by hand, relying on the prevailing winds to carry the gas towards Allied lines. Because of this method of dispersal, a large number of German soldiers were injured or killed in the process of carrying out the attack.

On 22 April it was a fine spring day with no abnormal activity noticed by the Allies. There was some shelling of Ypres in the late morning which gradually ceased. At 5pm a sudden bombardment opened from the German heavy artillery on the town and the villages in front of the town, almost untouched until now. Simultaneously the French field guns north-east

GAS

In the first gas attack on the Western Front on 22 April 1915, the gas used was chlorine – a choking agent that stripped the lining from the bronchial tubes and lungs, producing massive amounts of phlegm and a condition known as 'dry land drowning' in which the lungs fill with fluid. Mild inhalation produces vomiting and diarrhoea. Survivors cough up lung detritus for extended periods and lung damage is permanent with casualties requiring extensive medical treatment.

It was discovered that the gas hung low on the ground and consequently men who took cover at the bottom of trenches were at greater risk than those who manned the firing step. Gas would hang in pockets at the bottom of shell holes and men taking cover from artillery or small arms fire could fall victim to it. The surprise use of poison gas was not a historical first (poison gas had already been used on the Eastern Front) but did come as a tactical surprise to the Allies. Chlorine was a tricky agent to use so both sides developed more sophisticated gas weapons, and countermeasures, but after the Second Battle of Ypres never again was the use of gas either a surprise, nor especially effective. Indeed some soldiers said a gas attack was not entirely bad because it killed off the rats in the trenches.

Countermeasures were quickly introduced in response to the use of chlorine. The Germans issued their troops with small gauze pads filled with cotton waste, and bottles of a bicarbonate solution with which to dampen the pads. Immediately following the first gas attack, instructions were sent to British and French troops to hold handkerchiefs or cloths moistened with water or urine over their mouths. Simple pad respirators, similar to those issued to German troops, were soon proposed by Lieutenant Colonel N.C. Ferguson. These pads were intended to be used damp, preferably dipped into a solution of bicarbonate kept in buckets in the trenches. Because such pads could not be expected to arrive at the front for several days, many divisions set about making them for themselves.

35. *Later in the war canaries were used to detect poisonous gases, as they are extremely sensitive to such odours. (Birds and the War, Skeffington & Son, London, 1919; www.gwpda.org/photos)*

of Ypres began rapid fire, although the German field artillery remained silent. Then British lookouts saw two greenish-yellow clouds on the ground, on either side of Langemarck, in front of the German frontline. The clouds spread laterally and joined up, moving forward towards the Allied lines.

Initially the rolling cloud of yellowy vapour, with a smell like concentrated bleach, was assumed to be a smokescreen or possibly some type of tear gas. Approximately 6,000 French and Colonial troops, who were engulfed in the cloud, died within 10 minutes, primarily from asphyxiation and subsequent tissue damage in the lungs. Many more were blinded. Terrified, many of the French troops ran for the rear, not realising that as they ran the cloud moved with them. What compounded the terror caused by this weapon was that within 15 minutes it marked and etched metal and even caused rifles and artillery to jam.

Private W.A. Quinton of the 2nd Battalion, Bedfordshire Fusiliers painted a grim picture of the impact of the gas attack:

Men came stumbling from the front line. I've never seen men so terror stricken, they were tearing at their throats and their eyes were glaring out. Blood was streaming from those who were wounded and they were tumbling over one another. Those who fell couldn't get up because of the panic of the men following them, and eventually they were piled up two or three high in this trench.

from *Forgotten Voices of the Great War*

Chlorine gas forms hydrochloric (muriatic) acid when it is combined with water so in the human body it destroys moist tissues such as lungs and eyes. The chlorine gas, being denser than air, quickly flowed down into the trenches, forcing the troops to climb out into heavy enemy fire.

Corporal Charlie Parke of 2nd Battalion, Gordon Highlanders recalled the horrific death that followed a fatal dose of chlorine gas:

Men would claw at their throats in a futile attempt at relief, while their brass buttons were chemically converted to green by the action of the chloride. Their bodies swelled as they writhed on the ground in agony, their tongues hanging out; a bullet at this stage, whether of German or British origin, would have constituted a merciful escape.

from *The Soldier's War*

Wilfred Owen, who would die on 4 November 1918 just a week before the Armistice, describes the horrifying death of a soldier from gas in his poem *Dulce et Decorum Est*. The words in the poem '*Dulce et decorum est pro patria mori*' (It is sweet and right to die for your country) are taken from an ode by the ancient Greek poet Horace. However, death at Ypres on 22 April was neither sweet nor right.

With the survivors abandoning their positions en masse, a 4-mile (6.4km) gap was left in the frontline. However, the German High Command had not foreseen the effectiveness of their new weapon, and so had not put any reserves ready in the area to follow up the breakthrough, and Canadian troops were able to adopt improvised protection by urinating into cloths and covering their faces to counter the effects of the gas. Canadians held that part of the line against further attacks until 3 May 1915, at a cost of 6,000 wounded or dead. Casualties were especially heavy for the 13th Battalion (Royal Highlanders of Canada) CEF, which was enveloped on three sides and overextended by the demands of securing its left flank once the Algerian Division had broken.

However, in the French sector the Germans had stormed through Langemarck village and on into the opening gap left by the gas cloud. The quick thinking of the GOC of the 3rd Canadian Brigade, Brigadier General R.E.W. Turner VC, who, as soon as the attack started, had ordered up the reserve 14th Battalion at St Jean and counterattacked the advancing Germans near his headquarters at Mousetrap Farm. To the immediate left of the Canadians the French 1st Battalion, 1st Algerian Tirailleurs (light infantry) Division were unaffected by the gas and remained in position.

German troops started to enter the gap after 5pm in some numbers, but with the coming of darkness and the lack of follow-up troops the German forces were unable to exploit the opportunity to force a breakthrough. Near St Julien the oncoming Germans were held by two platoons of the 13th Canadian Battalion, which fought until the last man had fallen, and a company of the 14th Battalion. The Germans were finally stopped, at about 6.30pm, by two guns of the 10th Canadian Battery firing at short range.

Turner continued to organise reinforcements now arriving from the direction of Ypres, confirming that his original line was still in place. The Canadians threw in their reserve battalions as the Germans, unable to force a way across the Ypres–Poelcapelle road, continued to drive towards the Yser Canal. At 9pm it became clear to Plumer that the French collapse had been so complete that the gap in the Allied line was not 3,000 yards wide, but 8,000 yards. Almost simultaneously it was realised that the Germans had stopped advancing and were digging in. The prompt action of the Canadians in securing their flank and the German pause as night fell gave the Allies time to assess the situation and bring up fresh troops to fill the gap from the original Canadian left to the Yser Canal.

Private Underwood of the 1st Canadian Division recalled that the Canadian troops received orders to fire on the fleeing Algerian troops, who, to the surprise of the Canadians, were dressed in almost Napoleonic uniforms of blue coats, red trousers and caps; 1,000 of these 'original' troops were killed and 4,975 were wounded from an initial strength of 10,000.

In order to plug the gap created by the gas attack at Kitchener's Wood, the 10th Battalion, 2nd Canadian Brigade was ordered to counterattack. It would be a brave but doomed action. They formed up after 11pm on April 22 with 16th Battalion – Canadian Scottish of 3rd Brigade arriving off the march straight onto the start line with orders to support the advance. Without any reconnaissance, both battalions moved off at 11.46pm and over 800 men were formed up in waves of two companies each. The men soon encountered obstacles and the Germans opened up heavy machine gun fire. With remarkable courage the men broke into a run and with fixed bayonets cleared the shell-shattered wood, but at a cost of 75 per cent casualties. Before daylight on the 23rd the gap was covered by some ten battalions of troops with a further three and a half battalions in reserve.

The Canadian actions during the Battle of Gravenstafel are commemorated with the Saint Julien or Juliaan Memorial in the village of Sint Juliaan. The memorial 'Brooding Soldier' which shows the head and shoulders of a soldier with his rifle reversed (the drill position for a guard at a funeral) is the work of Frederick Chapman Clemesha and was selected to serve as the monument following a design competition organised by the Canadian Battlefield Monument Commission in 1920.

A powerful French memorial put up after the war on the site of the first gas attack showing men dying from chlorine inhalation was blown up by the Germans in 1940 because they found it distasteful.

36. Towering over the road junction at St Julien the statue of the Brooding Soldier is a powerful memorial to the heroic fight put up by Canadian troops of the CEF in the first gas attack of the war.

37. The statue shows a soldier with arms reversed – the soldier has his head lowered and his hands resting on the butt of his rifle – the drill position adopted by troops lining the route of a funeral.

St Julien

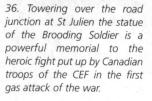

22 April Lance Corporal Fisher and fellow soldiers of 13th Battalion, Royal Canadian Highlanders, cover the retreat of Major King's field battery at St Julien; Fisher is awarded VC for the action

24 April Germans unleash another chlorine gas attack, west of St Julien

Canadian troops are overwhelmed; Germans take St Julien

25 April York and Durham Brigade, Northumberland Division counterattack and establish new line close to the village

Following the gas attack the village of St Julien, which had been in the rear of the 1st Canadian Division, had become part of the frontline. Individuals and small groups held the village and one

THE COLT 'POTATO DIGGER'

The Colt Model 1895 machine gun with which
Lance Corporal Fisher won his Victoria Cross was an
American-designed, gas-operated, belt-fed, air-cooled
automatic weapon. Though it had the Colt name, it
was designed during 1891–95 by the highly talented
John Moses Browning. It used a heavy, fixed barrel
and an unusual gas system with swinging gas piston.
In this system, the gas piston was located below
the barrel at the right angle to the bore, and upon
discharge it was blown by the powder gases down
and to the rear, pivoting on the long lever attached
to the barrel behind the port. This piston lever was
connected to the bolt by the set of struts and levers,
which transferred radial movement of the piston to
the linear movement of the bolt. This system required
sufficient clearance below the gun to operate,
otherwise the gun would literally dig into the ground,
thus earning the name of 'potato digger'.

such individual was Lance Corporal Frederick Fisher of the 13th
(Royal Canadian Highlanders) Battalion. He would win the VC on
April 22 when he twice went out with a handful of men and a
Colt machine gun and prevented advancing German troops from
capturing an artillery battery and passing through St Julien and
into the rear of the Canadian frontline. Fisher would be killed a
day later. Like so many VCs won in the First World War the simple
account of his action taken from the citation does not do credit to
the courage and determination of this NCO.

On 22 April Fisher was coming forward from St Julien when
he discovered some of the guns of Major W.B.M. King's field
battery were being fired upon by German infantry located very
close to them. It seemed the capture of these guns was imminent,
but Fisher set up his machine gun in advance of the battery, and
with the assistance of a few men, held off the Germans until the
guns were got away. During this encounter Fisher's small section

38. Rifleman F. Hamilton of 8th Rifle Brigade mans a Vickers machine gun during fighting near Hooge in July 1915. The Vickers was a robust, reliable weapon that would serve with the British Army through both the First and Second World Wars into the early 1960s.

was under intense fire and four of his six men were killed. Lance Corporal Fisher returned to St Julien.

Meanwhile Lieutenant Ross, with his machine guns, made a determined effort to cut down the enfilade fire that was causing the battalion such heavy losses. Ross was accompanied by Lance Corporal Fisher, who crawled out of a shallow trench and, setting up a gun, was shot dead. A moment later Sergeant McLeod, who had taken Fisher's place, was killed in the same way. Leaving this particular gun, Lieutenant Ross crawled to a spot where he ordered Lance Corporal Parkes and Private Glad to set up another gun and open fire. From this location he gained the advantage over the most devastating fire from the German trenches and maintained the Canadian superiority for the rest of the day. Fisher's was the first of seventy Canadian VCs awarded in the First World War.

The Germans released another cloud of chlorine gas on the morning of 24 April, directly towards the reformed Canadian lines just west of the village of St Julien. When the Canadians saw the approach of the greenish-grey gas cloud, the order was given to moisten their handkerchiefs with urine and cover their noses and mouths. These improvised countermeasures were ineffective and the Canadians were overwhelmed, allowing German troops to take the village.

During the fighting a young Canadian Lieutenant, Edward Bellew of the 7th (1st British Columbia) Battalion, would win the VC when he sited his machine gun on high ground to give it a better field of fire and engaged the men of the German 51st Division as they assaulted the Canadian lines. When the gun was smashed the officer fired relays of loaded rifles handed to him until he was wounded and taken prisoner. The Germans sentenced him to death on the grounds that he had continued to fire after part of his unit had surrendered. Even though he protested that he had not broken the rules of war a firing squad formed up but at the last minute his sentence was commuted. He remained a prisoner of war until 1919.

Men of the York and Durham Brigade, part of the Northumberland Division, counterattacked on the following day and though they failed to secure their objectives they established a new line close to the village. On the third day the 50th (Northumbrian) Division TF attacked again but with the loss of more than 1,900 men and 40 officers – two thirds of its strength – and only held part of the village before they were forced back.

It was during fighting on 2 May at Wieltje, a location known to the soldiers as 'Suicide Corner', that 28-year-old Londoner Private John 'Jacky' Lynn of 2nd Battalion, the Lancashire Fusiliers would literally give his life to save those of his comrades.

The Germans had put in an attack following the release of gas. Lynn, although almost overcome, continued to man his

39. Forty-year-old Jemadar Mir Dast of the 55th Coke's Rifles (Frontier Force) would win the VC in fighting on 26 April 1915 in the Second Battle of Ypres. He survived the war and died in India in June 1950.

machine gun. As the Germans closed with the trenches Lynn moved the machine gun onto the parapet so that he could fire more effectively. In the words of his citation: 'This eventually checked any further advance and the outstanding courage displayed by this soldier had a great effect upon his comrades in the very trying circumstances'. In reality Lynn was dying and he knew it as he kept fighting, his face had turned black and when the Germans had withdrawn, gasping for breath his last words to a fellow soldier before he died were 'This is the last carry, Flash'.

Private Alfred Bromfield interviewed long after the war recalled the single-handed stand by Lynn:

He was out to the right of our lines in a position where he could enfilade the whole ground in front of the German trenches, and he'd worked his machine gun the whole time. He was on his own, because his number two and three had already conked out with the gas. So he was firing on his own and they had to drag him off that gun – actually pull him away from it.

from *Forgotten Voices of the Great War*

Lynn would be awarded a posthumous Victoria Cross.

In the fighting the 2nd Battalion, Royal Dublin Fusiliers suffered heavily in the next two subsidiary battles at Frezenberg and Bellewaarde, with no respite. On 24 May the battalion was subject to a German chlorine gas attack near St Julien and effectively disintegrated as a fighting unit.

Frezenberg

4–7 May		Germans group three corps opposite British 27th and 28th divisions, near the Frezenberg Ridge
	5.30am	Germans launch artillery barrage on Frezenberg Ridge
8 May		British resist first and second assaults on their positions, but are forced to fall back during a third assault
		2-mile wide gap in the British line is opened up
		10th Brigade advance during the night to stabilise positions in the line
9 May		German troops attack 27th Division along the Menin Road, but achieve little
		German 39th Division breaks 7th Cavalry Brigade's front, forcing them to withdraw
13 May		British reinforcements and counterattacks restore the front

In the period 4–7 May, the German Fourth Army Commander Field Marshal Albrecht, Duke of Württemberg, had been encouraged by

40. A British infantry shelter in Ploegsteert Wood in 2011, the sand bags that served as shuttering when the concrete was poured have rotted away, but their outline remains. The rich moss covering has softened the outline of what must have been a claustrophobic and cramped shelter.

the British withdrawal following the use of gas and he ordered his artillery forward and grouped three corps opposite the weakened British 27th and 28th divisions holding the Frezenberg Ridge to the east of Ypres. Many of the British positions were unfinished with narrow trenches, some of which were only 3ft deep. Defence stores like sandbags, corrugated iron or barbed wire were restricted. Some positions on the forward edge of the Frezenberg Ridge and around Bellewaarde Lake were exposed to direct artillery and small arms fire. The 27th and 28th divisions had been unable to dig communications trenches or construct dug outs.

It was against this poorly prepared line that at 5.30am on 8 May German artillery opened up a brutal barrage, concentrating on the 83rd Brigade positions on the forward slopes of the ridge. Incredibly the German assault that followed was repelled by the battered battalions and a second assault was held, but a third directed at the flanks of Frezenberg village forced the British back. The German attack on the right against 80th Brigade was held, but 84th Brigade had been almost destroyed and a 2-mile wide gap torn in the British lines. Tenacious defence, hastily improvised counterattacks and, crucially, the night advance of 10th Brigade stabilised the situation.

The next day, 9 May, saw new German attacks further south against the 27th Division covering the Menin Road. Again despite heavy bombardment the German assaults that were spread over three days made no inroads. However, on 13 May, a day of heavy rain and artillery fire the German 39th Division broke into the 7th Cavalry Brigade's front, causing temporary withdrawals. Once again support troops came forward and counterattacks restored the front – albeit at a heavy price. In six days of intense fighting the German XV Corps had gained about 1,000 yards between Hooge and Mousetrap Farm, but the cost in casualties was so high that attacks were halted. On 10 May a final attack backed by gas was launched, but made little progress. When the battle ended German gains were 2,000 yards.

Bellewaarde

24 May	2.45am	Germans launch heavy bombardment against V Corps
		Germans release chlorine gas along the British frontline, allowing Germans to capture Mousetrap Farm
		British, unable to regain Mousetrap Farm, defend positions at Bellewaarde Lake
		84th Brigade forces Germans to withdraw from Witte Poort Farm
	11pm	80th Brigade and 84th Brigade launch counterattack, with heavy losses
	25 May	Battle stabilises and attacks cease

At 2.45am on 24 May, German artillery opened up a very heavy bombardment against the British V Corps' front. Mixed in with

41. In an almost Napoleonic scene near Shell Trap Farm – aka Mouse Trap Farm – men of 1st Battalion The King's Own (Royal Lancaster Regiment) led by 2nd Lieuteant R.C. Leach launch a counterattack and capture a German flag on 24 May 1915.

suppressive small arms fire they also released chlorine gas on almost the entire length of the British line. German infantry followed up the gas cloud and although the wind blowing from east to west had alerted the British that a gas attack might be launched, the speed of the attack caught them off their guard. Many men were struggling with their rudimentary respirators and large numbers were overcome. However they were able to give effective fire except at a ruined farm, nicknamed Mousetrap Farm, held by two platoons of the Royal Dublin Fusiliers and only 30 yards from the German trenches. It was quickly overrun.

Mousetrap Farm had been an attractive moated farm with outbuildings, now blasted and burned out, soldiers had given it the grim but accurate nickname of 'Shell Trap Farm'. British staff decided the name was bad for morale and on maps and in orders it was referred to as 'Mouse Trap Farm'.

Heroic efforts were made to recapture the farm but by evening it was decided that it was better to withdraw to a more defensible line. Corps reserve troops were committed to block the German breakthrough around Bellewaarde Lake, but this took time and the understrength frontline battalions had to hang on until early evening when the weakened 84th Brigade was able to attack and eject the Germans from Witte Poort Farm.

Following the belated arrival of 80th Brigade a joint night counterattack was launched after 11pm. Both battalions suffered badly in the assault that was launched in bright moonlight. The battle quietened in the early hours of the morning and a day later shelling fell off and the Germans launched no further attacks.

In late May after over four and a half weeks of savage and near continuous fighting the Second Battle of Ypres staggered to a close. The Allied defenders and German attackers were exhausted and punch drunk from the fighting. BEF casualties were over 59,000 killed, wounded and missing. The French had lost 10,000 while German losses are estimated at around 35,000. The shape of the Ypres Salient was now even harder to defend and the town was a constant target for German artillery. The situation would remain unchanged until the major British offensive in the summer of 1917.

The Second Battle of Ypres is forever associated with the German employment of chemical weapons. Gas produced limited tactical success, generated outrage and was a propaganda 'own goal'. Moreover, the Allies were quick to retaliate and the British used gas at the Battle of Loos on 25 September 1915.

The Salient

In the First Battle of Ypres French, Belgian, British and German troops fought across relatively unspoiled countryside with woods, hedgerows and small villages. Drainage ditches were an obstacle. However, the nature of the fighting was what would be called in modern doctrine 'a meeting engagement', in other words forces in the open and on the move were encountering one another and manoeuvring and fighting. Villages provided cover and there was scope to outflank hostile forces.

WIPERS TIMES

The *Wipers Times* was a troop magazine, produced by men of the 12th Battalion, Sherwood Foresters, 24th Division. In early 1916, the battalion was stationed in the frontline at Ypres and when the men came across an abandoned printing press a sergeant who had been a printer in peacetime salvaged it and printed a sample page. The paper itself was named after the soldiers' corruption of the town of Ypres.

The editor was Captain (later Lieutenant Colonel) F.J. Roberts, the sub-editor was Lieutenant F.H. Pearson. Cartoonist E.J. Couzens created the ironic style of the newspaper by inventing a chinless platoon commander clutching his swagger stick and wondering 'Am I as offensive as I might be?'

The paper consisted of poems, reflections, wry in-jokes and lampoons of the military situation the division was in. In general the paper maintained a humorously ironic style reflected in this spoof property advertisement:

BUILDING LAND FOR SALE
BUILD THAT HOUSE ON HILL 60.
BRIGHT-BREEZY & INVIGORATING
COMMANDS AN EXCELLENT VIEW OF
HISTORIC TOWN OF YPRES
FOR PARTICULARS OF SALE
APPLY:- BOSCH & CO MENIN

The Race to the Sea and the creation of deep and elaborate trenches changed the character of the battlefield completely. The Ypres Salient solidified and became known as The Salient to many soldiers or simply to men faced by the challenge of pronouncing a foreign name – 'Wipers'.

To the analogy of the town being a cup, located in a saucer formed by the hills to the east and south, should be added that water drained from the rim of the saucer into a complex matrix of drainage ditches cut through the sticky Flanders clay. Once these

42. February 1918 – the war has only nine more months to run as this weary stretcher party walks along a duckboard track in the pulverised terrain at Ypres. To slip off a duckboard into a crater was to risk death by drowning in the bottomless mire.

ditches and culverts had been smashed by artillery fire the clay turned into a sticky, apparently bottomless, 'goo' that could suck a man down and drown him.

Paths through the mud were made using slatted wooden walkways known as duckboards. These were used to line the bottom of trenches so water drained through the slats to sumps below. Duckboards were fine in dry weather, but they soon became slippery after rain and the passage of troops in muddy boots. Shell fire also smashed duckboards and they canted at an angle, and one soldier remembered that a gap had been filled by the bodies of two dead German soldiers. To slip off duckboards, particularly at night, into muddy bottomless craters was to be condemned to a ghastly death by drowning and there are numerous accounts of

DUCKBOARDS

Duckboards, slatted wooden walkways about two metres long and half a meter wide were used to line the bottom of trenches; as the water level was very high in the Ypres Salient these were regularly flooded. The boards helped to keep the soldiers' feet dry and prevent the development of the fungal condition known as Trench Foot caused by prolonged immersion in cold wet conditions. Duckboards also allowed for troops' easier movement through the trench systems. In the Ypres Salient, duckboards were laid at ground level over shell-cratered and muddy terrain to help soldiers moving up and down from the frontlines. Movement was often at night, but since duckboards were often slippery and could have shifted or been damaged by shell fire, falling or slipping off them could often be fatal as men drowned in what seemed like bottomless mud under the weight of their equipment. Today duckboards are used in communal shower blocks to ensure that water drains away.

soldiers pleading with mates to be shot in the head rather than die in such a manner. As one veteran explained if a man loaded up with a pack, weapon and ammunition was hit, he often fell forwards. It only needed a few inches of muddy water for a severely wounded man to drown. The body would then sink slowly into the mud. In the frontline Private James Racine of 1/5th Seaforth Highlanders would use water from a shell hole for washing and shaving. It was green and smelly but it:

> had to serve for ablution requirements. The water receded as the days passed, until one morning I discovered the body of a man at the bottom when I knelt down to wash; it occurred to me that the time had arrived when I should seek a more savoury position.
>
> from *The Soldier's War*

If the mud was not grim enough, newcomers were immediately struck by the appalling reek given off by numerous conflicting sources. Rotting bodies of men, mules and horses lay around in their thousands. Decaying flesh has a sickly sweet smell that pervades hair and clothing and would remain after men had come down from the line. Overflowing latrines would similarly give off a most offensive stench. Men who had not had a bath in weeks or months stunk of dried sweat. The feet were generally accepted to give off the worst odour.

Corporal Charlie Parke of 2nd Battalion, Gordon Highlanders watched death and decay with an almost forensic interest:

> In hot weather, the corpses of horses and men would swell up, although different parts to different extents. Fingers inflated only slightly, whereas stomachs swelled the most and, in fact, it was at this point that explosions would normally be expected to occur; in military bodies, however, the extremely strong webbing belt held the stomach in, so

43. A grim but evocative name for a little Commonwealth War Graves cemetery near Ploegsteert Wood, a shell-shattered wood known as 'Plug Street' to British soldiers. Cemeteries were also named after home town locations, logistic dumps and corps and regiments.

bursting occurred in two places, just above the belt and just below, near the crotch.

from The Soldier's War

Trenches would also smell of creosol or chloride of lime, used to stave off the constant threat of disease and infection. Add to this the smell of burned cordite, the lingering odour of poison gas, rotting sandbags, stagnant mud, cigarette smoke and cooking food. It was said that you could always tell if a man had come out of the line in the salient – it had its own unique smell that clung to their clothing and hair. Private C. Miles of the Royal Fusiliers recalled: 'You could smell a battalion coming out of the line if they were en masse and passed you close. A horrible smell of mud and corruption and unwashed bodies. It soaked right into you, that Ypres smell...'.

'I came to hate that salient. Absolutely loathed it. I always used to think the names were sinister – Zonnebeke – Hill 60 – Zillebeke – the names terrified you before you got there' remembered Lieutenant J.W. Naylor of the Royal Artillery.

The rats feasting off the bodies of men and horses grew as big as cats. They were a vile pest even in the town of Ypres, Gunner

44. The caption to this card reads 'Scotties have a clean up after a spell in the trenches' – the reality was that men stank, their clothing and bodies had lice, and it could be an effort to stay clean shaven, let alone clean.

Leonard Ounsworth of the Royal Garrison Artillery remembered:

> The rats used to pinch our rations at night... unless it was in
> a metal container. But the gas attack finished them. In the
> morning there were dozens and dozens of these rats crawling
> about on their bellies. We just stubbed our toe beneath them
> and sent them into the moat.

Looking back on his time in the Ypres Salient and the rats Private
Thomas McIndoe of 12th Battalion, Middlesex Regiment could
make light of the memories 'Rats! Oh Crikey! If they were put in
a harness they could have done a milk round, they were that big,
yes, honest… I used to line the sights up and give them one round
of ball. Bang! And blow them to nothing'.

*45. Pack mules loaded with shells are led off a 'corduroy road' – a
rudimentary wooden trackway onto a surfaced road. This picture taken
later in the war gives an idea of the mud and conditions under which men
and animals worked in the salient.*

AFTER THE BATTLE

The aftermath of the First and Second Battles of Ypres reflect the localised German gains made following the gas attack on the Allied left flank. When the front had stabilised following the mobile phase of First Ypres it ran just east of the Ypres Canal in the north, bulging eastwards towards Poelcappelle, southwards to Nieuwemolen and Molenaareslthoek, and then swung westwards around Polygon Wood down to Bass Wood and thence towards St Eloi. Ypres was now a classic salient, which according to the observer pointed towards the German-held railway junctions of Roulers and Comines, waiting to be cut off with attacks from the north and south, taking the key railway town of Ypres. Trenches, barbed wire and dug outs stabilised this line and the Germans were able to use the huge cement works at the occupied French city of Lille to build very solid bunkers – which with their reinforcing rods and bars look formidable even today.

The line changed following the Second Battle. Initially after the gas attack on 22 April 1915 there was a deep U-shaped dent on the left flank from Het Sas on the Ypres Canal to Langemarck. The front was now under 3 miles from Ypres. However, further pressure in the months that followed compressed the salient. By 24 May while the northern gains had not altered in the centre, the salient had been pushed back close to the Hooge Château, about

46. *A bunker integrated into the German trench system at Bayernwald. In many places the trenches have been returned to agricultural land and the bunkers survive in isolation. In reality all bunkers and strong points were linked into trench systems.*

2 miles from Ypres, and areas like Polygon Wood and Zonnebeke were in German hands.

The intensity of the artillery bombardment of Ypres reduced it to shell-shattered ruins. Happily for soldiers the cellars and basements remained and with the rubble of collapsed buildings above them were ideal shelters for troops transiting through the town. Though the demolished Cloth Hall would be the iconic image of Ypres, many soldiers found the destruction of the churches a source of deep offence.

The courage and prowess of the Canadian Division in Second Ypres had impressed the British and French. Another Canadian Division would join the BEF in late 1915 followed by two more in 1916.

The battle also blooded many commanders and some like the 6ft tall Brigadier Arthur Currie, would be tested and prove more than capable. He was commander of 2nd Brigade, 1st Division CEF – the division that had deployed to the Ypres Salient on 17 April 1915 and was faced by the German chemical warfare assault after less than a week in the line.

In the chaos that followed, Currie coolly issued orders from his headquarters, the much-battered Mousetrap Farm, even as it was gassed and then destroyed by fire. He was up against a situation not covered by any army training manual, but Currie cobbled together a fluid defence and counterattack that bent, but did not break. At one point he personally went back to the rear and brought up two regiments of British reinforcements. After several days of fierce fighting, Allied counterattacks re-established a stable defensive line, denying the Germans the breakthrough they had sought.

In some respects Currie resembles General William 'Bill' Slim, the British commander of the Fourteenth Army in Burma. Both had worked as schoolteachers before the First World War and had modest social backgrounds. Both had joined the volunteer part-time forces – the Militia in Canada and Territorial Force in Britain – and served as private soldiers and been promoted to corporal.

In 1900 Currie was offered an officer's commission, which would give him a much higher status in the social circles of Victoria. However he would be expected to pay for a tailored uniform and to give part of his pay to the officer's mess. In addition, Currie was engaged to be married to Lucy Chaworth-Musters. He changed career and accepted a commission and by 1914 held the rank of Brigadier.

However, the battles at Ypres had thrown up the inadequacies of training and doctrine in the early CEF, which were made obvious by the poor tactics used at Kitchener's Wood and St Julien.

THE WOODS OF THE WESTERN FRONT

'Woods' on the Western Front did not mean tall trees and sunlight dappling through rustling leaves. Artillery fire turned these areas into smashed stumps and twisted roots – they were both an obstacle and also an area into which troops could dig – but they certainly did not look like woods.

47. *Photographed in 1917 Ypres has become a shell-shattered ghost town – however the cellars still provided cover for troops transiting through the town. The Cloth Hall can be seen framed by the ruins in the foreground.*

At Second Ypres, the smallest tactical unit in the infantry had been a 100-man Company, but by 1917 it would be down to a ten-man section. In part Currie was responsible for these changes and though an aloof man he earned the respect of the soldiers under his command for his maxim 'Pay the price of victory in shells – not lives'.

The German forces had been commanded by Field Marshal Albrecht, Duke of Württemberg, who had been presented with a remarkable tactical opportunity by the gas attack that might have allowed his forces to break through to Ypres and beyond. It was the courage and flexibility of the Canadian and British soldiers that had denied him the victory.

48. An observer in a balloon took this picture of Ypres in 1917. It shows the random nature of destruction in war – while some buildings are wrecked beyond recognition others appear relatively undamaged.

The Ypres Salient continued to be a much-fought over area of the Western Front throughout the First World War, bearing witness to even more death and destruction during the later Battle of Passchendaele (or Third Battle of Ypres), from July to November 1917, amassing casualties of over 200,000 on each side.

The area surrounding Ypres still bears the scars of the three battles today and the countryside is dotted with many war graves, reminding the traveller that many young men lost their lives here.

THE LEGACY

The obvious legacy for any visitor to the Ypres Salient is the massive loss of life – cemeteries dot the slopes and nestle in woods, they are even to be found in the middle of the town itself. However there is a legacy that is not obvious but remains massively significant.

It was on the Ypres front that chemical weapons had first been used and it was here later in the war that Corporal Adolf Hitler was temporarily blinded by mustard gas. He described his personal experience in *Mein Kampf*:

During the night of October 13 to 14th [1918] the British opened an attack with gas on the front south of Ypres. They used the yellow gas whose effect was unknown to us, at least from personal experience. I was destined to experience it that very night. On a hill south of Werwick, in the evening of 13 October, we were subjected to several hours of heavy bombardment with gas bombs, which continued through the night with more or less intensity. About midnight a number of us were put out of action, some for ever. Towards morning I also began to feel pain. It increased with every quarter of an hour, and about seven o'clock my eyes were scorching as I staggered back and delivered the last dispatch I was destined to carry in this war. A few hours later my eyes were like glowing coals, and all was darkness around me…

from Adolf Hitler, *Mein Kampf*, Vol. 1, 1924

Hitler was evacuated to a hospital in Germany where as he was recovering he learned of the surrender of Imperial Germany. Mustard gas is a classified as a blister agent and has a nasty way of sticking to objects and equipment and producing injuries long after the initial attack is over.

It is perhaps ironic that mustard gas was a German development and was used for the first time by Germans in 1917 at Ypres. More than 14,000 British casualties were produced in the first three months and by the end of the First World War more than 120,000 British mustard casualties had occurred. The most commonly injured areas of the body were: eyes (86.1 per cent), respiratory tract (75.3 per cent), scrotum (42.1 per cent), face (26.6 per cent), anus (23.9 per cent), back (12.9 per cent), armpits (42.1 per cent), neck (12 per cent).

It was believed Hitler's experience of chemical attack in Ypres and the fear that the Allies might have similar weapons prompted him to ban the use of the much more deadly nerve agents: Tabun, Sarin and Soman. The agents had been developed in great secrecy by German chemists and weaponised in shells and bombs. Had they been employed the Allies would have had no protection against them, and since even minute quantities of nerve agents are lethal their employment could have radically changed the course of the Second World War.

Chemical weapons were used in some conflicts after the First World War but the most notorious was their employment by the Iraqis under Saddam Hussein in the war with Iran in the 1980s. Chemical weapons remain in the war stocks of some unstable nations and pose a threat to all the world.

FURTHER READING

Adcock, A St. John, For Remembrance, Soldier Poets Who Have Fallen in the War (Hodder & Stoughton, 1918)

Bruce, Anthony, An Illustrated Companion to the First World War (Michael Joseph Ltd, 1989)

Aitken, Sir Max, Canada in Flanders (Hodder & Stoughton, 1916)

Clayton, P.B., Tales of Talbot House, Everyman's Club in Poperinghe & Ypres 1915–1918 (Chatto & Windus, 1919), p. vii

Coombs, Rose E.B., Before Endeavours Fade (After the Battle Publications, 1990)

Dendooven, Dominiek, Menin Gate & Last Post (De Klaproos Editions, 2001 (English translation))

Duguid, Colonel A. Fortescue, and J.O. Patenaude, Official History of the Canadian Forces in The Great War 1914–1919, Volume I (I.S.O., 1938)

Edmonds, Brigadier General J.E., Military Operations: France and Belgium 1914, Volume I (Macmillan and Co. Ltd, 1922)

Edmonds, Brigadier General J.E., and Captain G.C. Wynne, Military Operations: France and Belgium 1915 (Macmillan and Co. Ltd, 1927)

Falkenhayn, General Erich von, General Headquarters 1914–1916 and its Critical Decisions (Hutchinson & Co, 1919 (English translation))

Fetherstonhaugh, F.C., 13th Battalion Royal Highlanders of Canada 1914–1919 (1925)

Graves, Dianne, A Crown of Life: The World of John McCrae (Spellmount Limited, 1997)

Haber, Ludwig Fritz, The Poisonous Cloud, Chemical Warfare in the First World War (Clarendon Press, 1986)

Harris, Robert, and Jeremy Paxman, A Higher Form of Killing, The Secret History of Gas and Germ Warfare (Random House, 2002)

Histories of Two Hundred and Fifty-One Divisions of the German Army which Participated in the War (1914–1918), Compiled from records of

Intelligence section of the General Staff, American Expeditionary Forces, at General Headquarters, Chaumont, France 1919 (London Stamp Exchange, 1989 [1920])

Hogg, Ian V., The Illustrated Encyclopedia of Artillery (Guild Publishing, 1987)

Keech, Graham, Battleground Europe Series: St. Julien (Ypres) (Leo Cooper, 2001)

McWilliams, James L., and R. James Steel, Gas! The Battle for Ypres, 1915 (Vanwell Publishing Ltd, 1985)

Patenaude, J.O., Official History of the Canadian Forces in The Great War 1914–1919, Volume I, Chronology, Appendices and Maps (I.S.O., 1938)

Pope, Stephen, and Elizabeth-Anne Wheal, The Macmillan Dictionary of The First World War (Macmillan, 1995)

Prescott, John F., In Flanders Fields, The Story of John McCrae (The Boston Mills Press, 1985)

Westman, Stephen, Surgeon with the Kaiser's Army (William Kimber, 1968) p. 57

ORDERS OF BATTLE

First Battle of Ypres

British Expeditionary Force (Sir John French)

I Corps (Haig)

1st Division (Lomax)
1st Guards Brigade
    1st Coldstream Guards
    1st Scots Guards
    1st Black Watch
    1st Queens Own
    Cameron Highlanders
    1st/14th Londons
    (London Scottish)
2nd Brigade
    2nd Royal Sussex
    1st Loyal North
    Lancashire
    1st Northamptonshire
    2nd The Kings Royal
    Rifle Corps
3rd Brigade
    1st The Queen's (Royal
    West Surrey)
    1st South Wales
    Borderers

    1st Gloucestershire
    2nd Welsh
XXV Brigade Royal Field
Artillery
    113th Battery
    114th Battery
    115th Battery
XXVI Brigade Royal Field
Artillery
    116th Battery
    117th Battery
    118th Battery
XXXIX Brigade Royal Field
Artillery
    46th Battery
    51st Battery
    54th Battery
XLIII (Howitzer) Royal Field
Artillery
    30th (Howitzer) Battery
    40th (Howitzer) Battery
    57th (Howitzer) Battery
    26th Heavy Battery
    Royal Garrison Artillery
Mounted Troops
    A Squadron, 15th
Hussars
    1st Cyclist Company

Engineers
- 23rd Field company Royal Engineers
- 26th Field company Royal Engineers

2nd Division (Monro)
4th Guards Brigade
- 2nd Grenadier Guards
- 2nd Coldstream Guards
- 3rd Coldstream Guards
- 1st Irish Guards
- 1st Hertfordshire

5th Brigade
- 2nd Worcestershire
- 2nd Oxfordshire and Buckinghamshire Light Infantry
- 2nd Highland Light Infantry
- 2nd Connaught Rangers

6th Brigade
- 1st The King's (Liverpool)
- 2nd South Staffordshire
- 1st Royal Berkshire
- 1st Kings Royal Rifle Corps

XXXIV Brigade Royal Field Artillery
- 22nd Battery
- 50th Battery
- 70th Battery

XXXVI Brigade Royal Field Artillery
- 15th Battery
- 48th Battery
- 71st Battery

XLI Brigade Royal Field Artillery
- 9th Battery
- 16th Battery
- 17th Battery

XLIV (Howitzer) Brigade Royal Field Artillery
- 47th (Howitzer) Battery
- 56th (Howitzer) Battery
- 60th (Howitzer) Battery

35th Heavy Battery Royal Garrison Artillery

Mounted Troops
- B Squadron, 15th Hussars
- 2nd Cyclist Company

Engineers
- 5th Field Company, Royal Engineers
- 11th Field Company, Royal Engineers

II Corps (Smith-Dorrien)

3rd Division (Hamilton)
7th Brigade
- 3rd Worcestershire
- 2nd South Lancashire
- 1st Wiltshire (Duke of Edinburgh's)
- 2nd Royal Irish Rifles

8th Brigade
- 2nd Royal Scots
- 2nd Royal Irish
- 4th Middlesex (Duke of Cambridge's Own)
- 1st Devonshire
- 1st Honourable Artillery Company

9th Brigade
- 1st Northumberland Fusiliers
- 4th Royal Fusiliers
- 1st Lincolnshire
- 1st Royal Scots Fusiliers

XXIII Brigade Royal Field Artillery
- 107th Battery
- 108th Battery
- 109th Battery

XL Brigade Royal Field Artillery
- 6th Battery
- 23rd Battery
- 49th Battery

XLII Brigade Royal Field Artillery
- 29th Battery

41st Battery
75th Battery
XXX (Howitzer) Brigade Royal Field Artillery
128th (Howitzer) Battery
129th (Howitzer) Battery
130th (Howitzer) Battery
48th Heavy Battery
Royal Garrison Artillery
Mounted Troops
C Squadron, 15th Hussars
3rd Cyclist Company
Engineers
56th Field Company, Royal Engineers
57th Field Company, Royal Engineers

5th Division (Fergusson)
13th Brigade
2nd Kings Own Scottish Borderers
2nd Duke of Wellington's Regiment (West Riding)
1st Royal West Kent
2nd The King's Own Yorkshire Light Infantry
14th Brigade
2nd Suffolk
1st East Surrey
1st Duke of Cornwall's Light Infantry
2nd Manchester
15th Brigade
1st Norfolk
1st Bedfordshire
1st Cheshire
1st Dorsetshire
XV Brigade Royal Field Artillery
11th Battery
52nd Battery
81st Battery
XXVII Brigade Royal Field

Artillery
119th Battery
120th Battery
121st Battery
XXVII Brigade Royal Field Artillery
122nd Battery
123rd Battery
124th Battery
VIII (Howitzer) Brigade Royal Field Artillery
37th (Howitzer) Battery
61st (Howitzer) Battery
65th (Howitzer) Battery
108th Heavy Battery
Royal Garrison Artillery
Mounted Troops
A Squadron, 19th Hussars
5th Cyclist Company
Engineers
17th Field Company, Royal Engineers
59th Field Company, Royal Engineers

III Corps (W. Pulteney)

4th Division (H.Wilson)
10th Brigade
1st Royal Warwickshire
2nd Seaforth Highlanders
1st Princess Victoria's (Royal Irish Fusiliers)
2nd Royal Dublin Fusiliers
11th Brigade
1st Prince Albert (Somerset Light Infantry)
1st East Lancashire
1st Hampshire
1st The Rifle Brigade
12th Brigade
1st The King's Own (Royal Lancaster)

2nd Lancashire Fusiliers
2nd Royal Inniskilling
Fusiliers
2nd Royal Sussex
XIV Brigade Royal Field Artillery
39th Battery
68th Battery
88th Battery
XXIX Brigade Royal Field
Artillery
125th Battery
126th Battery
127th Battery
XXXII Brigade Royal Field
Artillery
27th Battery
134th Battery
135th Battery
XXXVII (Howitzer) Brigade Royal
Field Artillery
31st (Howitzer) Battery
35th (Howitzer) Battery
55th (Howitzer) Battery
31st Heavy Battery Royal
Garrison Artillery
Mounted Troops
A Squadron, 19th
Hussars
4th Cyclist Company
Engineers
7th Field Company,
Royal Engineers
9th Field Company,
Royal Engineers

6th Division (J.L. Keir)
16th Brigade
1st Buffs (East Kent
Regiment)
1st Leicestershire
1st King's (Shropshire
Light Infantry)
2nd York and Lancaster
17th Brigade
1st Royal Fusiliers (City

of London Regiment)
1st Prince of Wales'
(North Staffordshire
Regiment)
2nd Prince of Wales'
Leinster (Royal
Canadians)
3rd Rifle Brigade (The
Prince Consort's Own)
18th Brigade
1st Prince of Wales'
Own (West Yorkshire
Regiment)
1st East Yorkshire
2nd Sherwood Foresters
(Nottinghamshire and
Derbyshire Regiment)
2nd Durham Light
Infantry
19th Brigade
2nd Royal Welsh
Fusiliers
2nd Queen's Own
Cameron Highlanders
1st Middlesex
2nd Argyll and
Sutherland Highlanders
II Brigade Royal Field Artillery
21st Battery
42nd Battery
53rd Battery
XXIV Brigade Royal Field
Artillery
110th Battery
111th Battery
112th Battery
XXXVIII Brigade Royal Field
Artillery
24th Battery
34th Battery
72nd Battery
XII (Howitzer) Brigade Royal
Field Artillery
43rd (Howitzer) Battery
86th (Howitzer) Battery

87th (Howitzer) Battery
24th Heavy Battery
Royal Garrison Artillery
Mounted Troops
    C Squadron, 19th
    Hussars
    6th Cyclist Company
Engineers
    12th Field Company,
    Royal Engineers
    38th Field Company,
    Royal Engineers

Royal Flying Corps (D. Henderson)
HQ Wireless Unit
2nd, 3rd, 4th, 5th and 6th
Aeroplane Squadrons (sixty-three machines)

Cavalry Corps (Allenby)

1st Cavalry Division (H. de Lisle)
    2nd Dragoon Guards
    5th Dragoon Guards
    11th Hussars
    1st Signal Troop
2nd Cavalry Brigade
    4th Dragoon Guards
    9th Lancers
    18th Hussars
    2nd Signal Troop
VIII Brigade Royal Horse Artillery
    Battery I
    Battery L
Cavalry Divisional Troops
    1st Field Squadron Royal
    Engineers
    1st Signal Squadron
    1st Cavalry Division
    supply column
    1st and 3rd Cavalry Field
    Ambulances

2nd Cavalry Division (H. Gough)
3rd Cavalry Brigade

4th Hussars
5th Lancers
16th Lancers
3rd Signal Troop
4th Cavalry Brigade
    6th Dragoon Guards
    3rd Hussars
    Composite Regiment of
    Household Cavalry
    4th Signal Troop
5th Cavalry Brigade
    2nd Dragoons
    12th Lancers
    20th Hussars
    5th Signal Troop
II Brigade Royal Horse Artillery
    Cavalry Divisional Troops
    2nd Field Squadron
    Royal Engineers
    2nd Signal Squadron
    2nd Cavalry Division
    supply column
    2nd, 4th and 5th Cavalry
    Field Ambulances

IV Corps (H. Rawlinson)

7th Division (T. Capper)
20th Brigade
    1st Grenadier Guards
    2nd Scots Guards
    2nd Border
    2nd Gordon
    Highlanders
21st Brigade
    2nd Bedfordshire
    2nd Green Howards
    (Alexandra, Princess of
    Wales's Own Yorkshire
    Regiment)
    2nd Royal Scots Fusiliers
    2nd Wiltshire (Duke of
    Edinburgh's)
22nd Brigade
    2nd Queen's (Royal
    West Surrey)

2nd Royal Warwickshire
1st Royal Welsh Fusiliers
1st South Staffordshire
XIV Brigade Royal Horse Artillery
XXII Brigade Royal Field Artillery
XXXV Brigade Royal Field Artillery
24th Heavy Brigade Royal Garrison Artillery
7th Divisional ammunition column
Mounted Troops
    Northumberland Hussars
    7th Cyclist Company
Engineers
    54th Field Company, Royal Engineers
    55th Field Company, Royal Engineers
Divisional Troops
    7th Signal Company
    7th Divisional Train
    21st, 22nd and 23rd Field Ambulances

3rd Cavalry Division (J. Byng)
6th Cavalry Brigade
    3rd (Prince of Wales') Dragoon Guards
    1st Royal Dragoons
    10th Hussars
7th Cavalry Brigade
    1st Life Guards
    2nd Life Guards
    Royal Horse Guards
XV Brigade Royal Horse Artillery
Cavalry Divisional Troops
    3rd Field Squadron Royal Engineers
    3rd Signal Squadron
    33rd Cavalry Division supply column

    6th and 7th Cavalry Field Ambulances

Indian Corps (J. Willcocks)

Lahore Division (H.B.B. Watkins)
Ferozepore Brigade
    1st Connaught Rangers
    9th Bhopal Infantry
    57th Wilde's Rifles
    129th Duke of Connaught's Own Baluchis
Jullundur Brigade
    1st Manchester
    15th Ludhiana Sikhs
    47th Sikhs
    59th Scinde Rifles

Meerut Division (C.A. Anderson)
Dehra Dun Brigade
    1st Coldstream Guards
    6th Jat Light Infantry
    2/2 King Edward VII's Own Gurkha Rifles (The Sirmoor Rifles)
    1/9 Gurkha Rifles
Garwhal Brigade
    2nd Leicestershire
    1/39 Garhwal Rifles
    2/39 Garhwal Rifles
    2/3 Queen Alexandra's Own Gurkha Rifles
Bareilly Brigade
    2nd Black Watch
    41st Dogras
    58th Vaughan's Rifles
    2/8 Gurkha Rifles
IV Brigade Royal Field Artillery
IX Brigade Royal Field Artillery
XIII Brigade Royal Field Artillery
    110th Heavy Battery Royal Garrison Artillery
Meerut Divisional ammunition column

Mounted Troops
- 4th Cavalry (Lancers)

Engineers
- 3rd Company, 1st King George V's Own Bengal Sappers and Miners
- 4th Company, 1st King George V's Own Bengal Sappers and Miners

Divisional Troops
- Meerut Signal Company
- 107th Pioneers
- Meerut Divisional Train
- 19th and 20th Field Ambulances
- 128th, 129th and 130th (Indian) Field Ambulances

French Eighth Army (d'Urbal)

IX Corps (Dubois)

17th Division (Guignabautdet)
18th Division (Lefevre)
6th Cavalry Division (Requichot)
7th Cavalry Division (Hely d'Oissel)

XVI Corps (Grossetti)

32nd Division (Bouchez)
43rd Division (Lanquetot)
39th Division (Danant)
31st Division (Vidal)

XXXII Corps (Humbert)

38th Division (Muteau)
42nd Division (Duchesne)
89th Territorial Division (Boucher)
4th Cavalry Division (Buyer)

XX Corps (Balfourier)

11th Division (Ferry)

26th Division (Hallouin)
II Cavalry Corps (de Mitry)
87th Territorial Division (Roy)
5th Cavalry Division (Allenou)
9th Cavalry Division (de L'espee)
I Cavalry Corps (Conneau)
1st Cavalry Division (Mazel)
3rd Cavalry Division (Lastours)
10th Cavalry Division (Contades)

German Fourth Army (Albrecht)

III Reserve Corps (von Beseler)

5th Reserve Division
6 batteries, 6th Reserve Field Artillery Regiment
- 9th Reserve Infantry Brigade
- 8th Reserve Infantry Regiment
- 48th Reserve Infantry Regiment
- 10th Reserve Infantry Brigade
- 12th Reserve Infantry Regiment
- 52nd Reserve Infantry Regiment

6th Reserve Division
6 batteries, 6th Reserve Field Artillery Regiment
- 11th Reserve Infantry Brigade
- 20th Reserve Infantry Regiment
- 24th Reserve Infantry Regiment
- 12th Reserve Infantry Brigade
- 26th Reserve Infantry Regiment
- 35th Reserve Infantry Regiment

4th Ersatz Division
>9th Gemischte Ersatz-Brigade
>13th Gemischte Ersatz-Brigade
>33rd Gemischte Ersatz-Brigade

XXII Reserve Corps (von Falkenhayn)

43rd Reserve Division
85th Reserve Infantry Brigade
86th Reserve Infantry Brigade

44th Reserve Division
87th Reserve Infantry Brigade
88th Reserve Infantry Brigade

XXIII Reserve Corps (von Kleist)

45th Reserve Division
89th Reserve Infantry Brigade
90th Reserve Infantry Brigade

46th Reserve Division
91st Reserve Infantry Brigade
92nd Reserve Infantry Brigade

XXVI Reserve Corps (von Hügel)

51st Reserve Division
101st Reserve Infantry Brigade
102nd Reserve Infantry Brigade

52nd Reserve Division
103rd Reserve Infantry Brigade
104th Reserve Infantry Brigade

XXVII Reserve Corps (von Carlowitz)

53rd Reserve Division
105th Reserve Infantry Brigade
106th Reserve Infantry Brigade

54th Reserve Division
107th Reserve Infantry Brigade
108th Reserve Infantry Brigade

Marine Division

German Sixth Army (Rupprecht)

II Army Corps (von Linsingen)

30th Aviation Battalion
15th Foot Artillery Regiment (Heavy)

3rd Division
3rd Artillery Brigade
>3rd Horse Grenadiers
5th Infantry Brigade
>2nd Grenadier Regiment
>9th Grenadier Regiment
6th Infantry Brigade
>34th Fusilier Regiment
>42nd Infantry Regiment

4th Division
4th Artillery Brigade
>12th Dragoons
7th Infantry Brigade
>14th Infantry Regiment
>149th Infantry Regiment
8th Infantry Brigade
>49th Infantry Regiment
>140th Infantry Regiment

VII Army Corps (von Claer)

13th Division
25th Brigade
26th Brigade
13th Field Artillery Brigade

14th Division
27th Brigade
79th Brigade
14th Field Artillery Brigade

Orders of Battle

XIII Army Corps (von Fabeck)

26th Division
51st Brigade
52nd Brigade
26th Field Artillery Brigade

25th Reserve Division
49th Reserve Infantry Brigade
50th Reserve Infantry Brigade

XIX (Saxon) Corps (von Laffert)

24th Division
3rd Brigade
4th Brigade
2nd Field Artillery Brigade

40th Division
7th Brigade
8th Brigade
4th Field Artillery Brigade

XIV Reserve Corps (von Loden)

26th Reserve Division
51st Reserve Infantry Brigade
52nd Reserve Infantry Brigade

6th Bavarian Reserve Division
12th Bayerische Reserve
Infantry Brigade
14th Bayerische Reserve
Infantry Brigade

Other German Corps

XV Corps (von Deimling)

30th Division
60th Brigade
85th Brigade
30th Field Artillery Brigade

6th Bavarian Reserve Division
85th Brigade

30th Field Artillery Brigade

9th Division
61st Brigade
82nd Brigade
39th Field Artillery Brigade

39th Division
61st Brigade
82nd Brigade
39th Field Artillery Brigade

II Bavarian Corps (von Martini)

3rd Bavarian Division
4th Bavarian Division

Plettenberg's Corps (von Plettenberg)

39th Division
Composite Guard Division (Winkler)

I Cavalry Corps (von Richthofen)

Guard Cavalry Division (von Etzel)
4th Cavalry Division (von Garnier)
1 Cavalry Corps (von der Marwitz)
2nd Cavalry Division (von Neuberg)
7th Cavalry Division (von Heydebreck)
IV Cavalry Corps (von Hollen)
6th Cavalry Division (Egon von Smettow)
9th Cavalry Division (Eberhard von Smettow)

V Cavalry Corps (von Stetton)

3rd Cavalry Division (von Unger)
Bavarian Cavalry

Second Battle of Ypres

British Second Army (General Smith-Dorrien)

As at outset of battle, brigade and divisional reserves not included.

V Corps (H. Plumer)

1st Canadian Division
1st Canadian Brigade
 1st (Western Ontario) Battalion
 2nd (Western Ontario) Battalion
 3rd (Toronto) Battalion
 4th Battalion
2nd Canadian Brigade
 5th (Western Cavalry) Battalion
 7th (1st British Columbia) Battalion
 8th (Winnepeg Rifles) Battalion
 10th Battalion
3rd Canadian Brigade
 13th (Royal Highlanders of Canada) Battalion
 14th (Royal Montreal) Battalion
 15th (48th Highlanders of Canada) Battalion
 16th (Canadian Scottish) Battalion

Canadian Field Artillery
2nd Brigade
 5th Battery
 6th Battery
 7th Battery
 8th Battery
3rd Brigade
 9th Battery
 10th Battery
 11th Battery
 12th Battery

27th Division
80th Brigade
 Princess Patricia's Canadian Light Infantry
 3rd Battalion, King's Royal Rifle Corps
 4th Battalion, King's Royal Rifle Corps
81st Brigade
 1st Battalion, Argyll & Sutherland Highlanders
 9th Battalion, Argyll & Sutherland Highlanders
 1st Battalion, Royal Scots
82nd Brigade
 2nd Battalion, Royal Irish Fusiliers
 1st Battalion, the Cambridgeshire Regiment
 1st Battalion, the Leinster Regiment

28th Division
83rd Brigade
 2nd Battalion, the King's Own Regiment
 3rd Battalion, the Monmouthshire Regiment
 1st Battalion, the King's Own Yorkshire Light Infantry
84th Brigade
 1st Battalion, the Welsh Regiment
 12th Battalion, the London Regiment

1st Battalion, the Suffolk Regiment.
85th Brigade
    3rd Battalion, Royal Fusiliers
    2nd Battalion, East Surrey Regiment.

27th Division Field Artillery
28th Division Field Artillery

French Army Détachement d'Armée de Belgique (General Putz)

Groupement d'Elverdinghe

45th (Algerian) Division
    90th Brigade
    91st Brigade

87th Territorial Division
    173rd Brigade
    174th Brigade
    186th Brigade

German Fourth Army (Albrecht)

XXIII Reserve Corps

45th Reserve Division
    89th Reserve Brigade
    90th Reserve Brigade
    17th Reserve Jäger Battalion

46th Reserve Division
    91st Reserve Brigade
    92nd Reserve Brigade
    18th Reserve Jäger Battalion

XXVI Reserve Corps

51st Reserve Division
    101st Reserve Brigade
    102nd Reserve Brigade
    23rd Reserve Jäger Battalion
    2nd Reserve Ersatz Brigade

52nd Reserve Division
    103rd Reserve Brigade
    104th Reserve Brigade
    24th Reserve Jäger Battalion

XXVII Reserve Corps

38th Landwehr Brigade

53rd Reserve Division (Saxon)
    105th Reserve Brigade
    106th Reserve Brigade
    25th Reserve Jäger Battalion
54th Reserve Division (Württemberg)
    107th Reserve Brigade
    108th Reserve Brigade
    26th Reserve Jäger Battalion

XV Corps

30th Infantry Division
    60th Brigade
    85th Brigade
39th Infantry Division
    61st Brigade
    82nd Brigade

INDEX

Aisne, river 20, 22, 33, 47, 83
Allenby, General Edmund 40, 49, 52, 53, 86, 97,
Allfrey, 2nd Lieutenant Edward 115,
Anderson, General C.A., 54
Antwerp 23, 41, 54,
Armentieres, battle of 16
Balfourier, General Maurice 46, 115
Bass Wood 138
Bayernwald 55, 139
Becelaere 95, 99
Bellew, Lieutenant Edward, VC, 125
Bellewaarde 18, 127, 128, 129, 131
Bikschote 17, 18, 98
Biscoe, 2nd Lieutenant F.C.F., 89
Bowring, Captain E.L., 89
British Army formations:
    First Army 48, 53
    Second Army 49, 53, 111
    Fourth Army 39, 53
    I Corps 17, 47, 48, 84, 85, 92, 93, 95, 96, 97, 100
    II Corps 42, 48, 51, 52, 92, 93, 97, 101, 103
    IV Corps 17, 54, 95, 97
    V Corps 49, 111, 115, 129
    Cavalry Corps 52, 95
    Royal Artillery Corps 38, 36, 70, 77, 136
    Royal Flying Corps 96, 99

1st Cavalry Division 52, 92, 95, 111
2nd Cavalry Division 111
3rd Cavalry Division 54, 111
1st Infantry Division 48
2nd Division 48, 93, 96, 97, 99
3rd Infantry Division 51
3rd Lahore Division 54, 94
4th Division 111
5th Infantry Division 51, 92, 93, 94, 95
6th Division 92, 93,
7th Division 17, 23, 54, 81, 84, 86
7th Meerut Division 54
27th Division 111, 127, 129
28th Division 11
50th Lahore Division 111
129th Duke of Connaught's Own Baluchis 87, 90
171 Tunnelling Company 108
Royal Engineers 36, 72
Royal Naval Air Service 23
Royal Naval Division (RND) 23
British Expeditionary Force (BEF) 16, 22, 32, 33, 36, 47, 48, 49, 50, 54, 59, 68, 83, 85 96, 97, 104, 106, 116, 131, 139
Bromfield, Private Alfred 126

Broodseinde 17
Brussels 41
Byng, Major General Julian 54
Canadian Army formations:
    Canadian Machine Gun Corps 39
    1st Canadian Division 58, 111, 121, 122, 139
Canadian Expeditionary Force (CEF) 38, 113, 120, 139, 140
Capper, Major General Thompson 54, 95
Carey, Lieutenant Gordon 112
Chlorine Gas 76, 113, 116, 117, 119, 121, 122, 125, 127, 129, 130
Churchill, First Lord of the Admiralty, Winston 23
Clarke, Corporal 35
Cloth Hall, Ypres 17, 19, 20, 139, 141
Comines Canal 101, 104, 138
Commonwealth War Graves cemetery 11, 135
Conneau, General Louis 46, 97
Cook, Corporal Arthur 107
Currie, Brigadier Arthur 139–140
D'Oyly Snow, Lieutenant General Thomas 49
d'Urbal, General Victor Louis Lucien 46, 97, 98, 99, 100

Index

Dast, Jemadar Mir 126
Davies, Lieutenant Colonel
    Henry 103
de Lisle, General Sir Henry
    52, 95
de Mitry, General Antoine
    46, 99, 101
Dimmer, Lieutenant John,
    VC, 105
Dixmude 97, 99, 101, 102
Dubois, General Pierre 46,
    100
Dwyer, Private E., VC, 110
Fellowes, Major R.T., 107
Ferguson, Lieutenant Colonel
    N.C., 117
Fergusson, General Charles
    51
Fisher, Lance Corporal
    Frederick, VC, 122–125
French Army formations:
    Eighth Army 46, 97,
        98, 99
    I Cavalry Corps 46, 93,
        96, 97
    IX Corps 46, 100
    XIV Corps 17
    XVI Corps 46
    XX Corps 46, 115
    XXXII Corps 46
    7th Infantry Division 46
    11th Division 46
    17th Division 100, 101
    18th Infantry Division
        46, 100
    26th Division 46
    31st Infantry Division 46
    32nd Infantry Division 46
    38th Territorial Division 46
    39th Infantry Division 46
    42nd Territorial Division
        46, 97, 99, 101
    43rd Infantry Division 46
    45th Algerian Division 46,
        111, 113
    87th Metropolitan
        Division 111
    87th Territorial Division
        46, 113
    89th Territorial Division 46
French, Field Marshal Sir John
    47, 48, 50, 84, 93, 97
Frezenberg, battle of 18,
    127, 128
Frezenberg Ridge 128
Geary, 2nd Lieutenant 110

German Army formations:
    First Army 41
    Fourth Army 41, 93, 96,
        101, 127
    Sixth Army 29, 43,
        45, 97
    Group Fabeck 45, 46
    Group Gerok 46, 101
    Group Herzog Albrecht
        40, 41
    Group Linsingen 45
    I Cavalry Corps 46, 97
    II Cavalry Corps 46
    IV Cavalry Corps 46, 97
    V Cavalry Corps 46, 97
    II Bavarian Corps 46
    III Reserve Corps 41, 97
    VII Corps 45, 97
    XIII Corps 45, 46, 93,
        97, 105
    XIV Corps 45
    XIX Corps ('Saxon') 45,
        97
    XV Corps 45, 46
    XV Corps 45, 85, 116,
        129
    XXII Corps 27
    XXII Reserve Corps 96,
        97
    XXIII Corps 27, 97, 99
    XXVI Corps 29
    XXVII Corps 29, 102
    XXVI Reserve Corps
        42, 97
    XXVII Reserve Corps 41
    Bavarian Cavalry Division
        46
    Guards Cavalry Division
        46
    3rd Bavarian Division 45
    3rd Infantry Division 42,
        101, 102
    3rd Reserve Division 46
    4th Bavarian Division 45
    4th Ersatz Division 41
    4th Infantry Division 42,
        46, 101, 103, 104
    5th Reserve Division 41
    6th Bavarian Reserve
        Division 29, 46, 84, 101
    6th Reserve Division 41
    9th Reserve Division 29
    13th Division 45
    14th Division 45
    24th Division 45
    25th Reserve Division 45,

46, 93, 101
    26th Division 45, 46,
        93, 102
    26th Reserve Division 45
    30th Division 45, 81, 86
    39th Division 45, 127, 129
    40th Division 45
    43rd Reserve Division
        27, 41
    44th Reserve Division
        27, 41
    45th Division 27
    46th Division 27
    46th Reserve Division 96
    51st Division 29, 125
    51st Reserve Division
        42, 114
    52nd Division 29
    52nd Reserve Division
        42
    53rd Division 29
    53rd Reserve Division 42
    54th Division 29
    54th Reserve Division 42,
        81, 86
    Prussian Guards Division
        46
    Marine Division 29
    German Air Service 96
Gheluvelt 16, 17, 28, 44,
    81, 84, 85, 87, 88, 89,
    90, 102
Gheluvelt Château 87, 89
Gheluvelt-Zandvoorde line
    81, 86
Gibbons, Corporal 72,
Gough, General Hubert
    52, 95
Gravenstafel 18, 113, 121
Griffiths, Major John Norton,
    MP, 107
Grossetti, General Paul 46,
    99
Haig, General Sir Douglas
    47, 48, 49, 50, 51, 52,
    84, 85, 86, 92, 93, 96,
    104
Hamilton, General Hubert 51
Hamilton, General Sir Ian 48
Hamilton, Rifleman F., 124
Hankey, Major E.B., 88–90
Het Sas 138
Hill 60 18, 108, 109, 110,
    111, 132, 136
Hitler, Adolf 44, 45, 99,
    143, 144

Hollebeke 81, 86, 92,
Hollebeke Château 92, 95
Hollen, Lieutenant General 46
Hooge 17, 18, 111, 112, 124, 129
Hooge Château 48, 138
Hooge Crater cemetery 86
Humbert, General Georges Louis 46
Hunter-Weston, Brigadier Aylmer 94
Jaeger, Private August 114, 116
Kaiser Wilhelm of Germany 32, 40, 41
Keir, General John 52, 93
Kemmel heights 86
Khan, Sepoy Khudadad, VC, 91–92
King, Major W.B.M., 123
Kitchener, Lord, Secretary of State for War 23, 24, 49, 50, 55, 59
Kitchener's Wood 113, 121, 140
Kortewilde 92, 95
Kruiseecke 95
La Bassee 83, 92, 93, 98
La Valle 92, 93
Langemarck 16, 17, 84, 97, 98, 99, 102, 113, 118, 120, 138
Le Cateau 49, 51, 68
Le Gheer 92, 94
Le Pilly 92, 93,
Leach, Colonel H.E. Burleigh 89
Leach, 2nd Lieutenant R.C., 130
McCrae, Lieutenant Colonel John 14, 15
Lille 26, 138
Lomax, Lieutenant General Samuel 47
Lynn, Private John 'Jacky' 125, 126, 127
Marne, battle of the 20, 40, 45, 47, 50, 51
Martin-Leake, Lieutenant Arthur, VC, 100
McIndoe, Private Thomas 137
Menin Gate Memorial to the Missing 11, 12, 13, 58
Menin Road 18, 84, 86, 101, 102, 127, 129
Messines 16, 81, 84, 86, 101

Messines Ridge 50, 92, 95
Miles, Private C., 136
Molenaareslthoek 138
Monro, Major General Charles Carmichael 48, 53, 103
Mons 33, 49, 50, 51, 68
Mousetrap Farm (Shell Trap Farm) 120, 129, 130, 140
Mustard Gas 143, 144
Naylor, Lieutenant J.W. 136
Neame, Sapper Captain Phillip 70
Newell, Corporal T., 108
Nieuport 99, 100, 101
Nieuwemolen 138
Nonnebosschen (Nun's Copse) 17, 101, 102, 103
Ostend 20, 23, 99
Ounsworth, Gunner Leonard 137
Parke, Corporal Charlie 23, 107, 119, 124, 135
Passchendaele 95
Passchendaele-Becelaere line 101
Ploegstreet ('Plug Street') 17, 128, 135
Plumer, General Hubert 48, 49, 116, 120
Poelcappelle 120, 138
Poezelhoek 93, 95
Polderhoek Ridge 88
Polygon Wood 87, 88, 89, 101, 102, 103, 138, 139
Racine, Private James 134
Rawlinson, General Henry 17, 40, 53
Reutel 101
Rijselpoort (Lille Gate), Ypres 19
Roulers 101, 114, 138
Roupell, Lieutenant 110
Rupprecht, Crown Prince of Bavaria 29, 42, 43
Smith-Dorrien, General Horace 48, 49, 51, 92, 93, 94, 97
St Eloi 17, 102, 138
St Jean 120
St Julien 17, 18, 120, 122, 123, 124, 125, 127, 140
St Martin's Church, Ypres 17, 52
Steenstraat 97, 99
Thomas, Captain Reginald 70
Thourout 93, 96, 101

Todd, Lieutenant J., 109
Turner, Brigadier General R.E.W., VC, 120
Tyne Cot Memorial to the Missing 13
Veldhoek 103
Verdun 13, 41
von Beseler, General Hans 39, 41, 105
von Carlowitz, General 42, 97
von Claer, General Eberhard 45
von Deimling, General Berthold 45
von Fabeck, General Gustav 45, 46
von Falkenhayn, General Erich 23, 41, 42
von Hugel, General 42
Von Kleist, General 96
von Kluck, General Alexander 41
von Laffert, General Maximilian 45
von Linsingen, General Adolf 45
von Loden, General 45
von Martini, General Karl 45
von Marwitz, General 46
von Plettenberg, General Karl 45
von Richthofen, General 46
von Schubert, General 42
von Wurttemberg, Field Marshal Albrecht Herzog, 29, 39, 40, 101, 104, 127, 141
Watkis, General H.B.B., 54, 94
Wieltje ('Suicide Corner') 125
Williamson, Rifleman Henry 34
Wilson, General Henry Fuller Maitland 52, 100
Witte Poort Farm 129, 131
Woolley, 2nd Lieutenant Geoffrey, VC, 110
Wytschaete 17
Ypres Canal 14, 138
Yser Canal 93, 96, 102, 120, 121
Zandvoorde 16, 81, 86
Zeebrugge 23, 54
Zillebeke 17, 81, 86, 91, 105, 116, 136
Zonnebeke 16, 17, 100, 136, 139
Zonnebeke Château 93, 95